Cambridge Elements ☰

Elements in Global China
edited by
Ching Kwan Lee
University of California, Los Angeles

GLOBAL CHINA AS METHOD

Ivan Franceschini
The Australian National University

Nicholas Loubere
Lund University

CAMBRIDGE
UNIVERSITY PRESS

CAMBRIDGE
UNIVERSITY PRESS

Shaftesbury Road, Cambridge CB2 8EA, United Kingdom

One Liberty Plaza, 20th Floor, New York, NY 10006, USA

477 Williamstown Road, Port Melbourne, VIC 3207, Australia

314–321, 3rd Floor, Plot 3, Splendor Forum, Jasola District Centre, New Delhi – 110025, India

103 Penang Road, #05–06/07, Visioncrest Commercial, Singapore 238467

Cambridge University Press is part of Cambridge University Press & Assessment, a department of the University of Cambridge.

We share the University's mission to contribute to society through the pursuit of education, learning and research at the highest international levels of excellence.

www.cambridge.org
Information on this title: www.cambridge.org/9781108995566
DOI: 10.1017/9781108999472

First published 2022

A catalogue record for this publication is available from the British Library.

ISBN 978-1-108-99556-6 Paperback
ISSN 2632-7341 (online)
ISSN 2632-7333 (print)

Cambridge University Press & Assessment has no responsibility for the persistence or accuracy of URLs for external or third-party internet websites referred to in this publication and does not guarantee that any content on such websites is, or will remain, accurate or appropriate.

Global China as Method

Elements in Global China

DOI: 10.1017/9781108999472
First published online: July 2022

Ivan Franceschini
The Australian National University

Nicholas Loubere
Lund University

Author for correspondence: Ivan Franceschini, franceschini.ivan@gmail.com

Abstract: Is China part of the world? Based on much of the political, media, and popular discourse in the West the answer is seemingly no. Even after four decades of integration into the global socio-economic system, discussions of China continue to be underpinned by a core assumption: that the country represents a fundamentally different 'Other' that somehow exists outside the 'real' world. Either implicitly or explicitly, China is generally depicted as an external force with the potential to impact on the 'normal' functioning of things. This core assumption, of China as an orientalised, externalised, and separate 'Other', ultimately produces a distorted image of both China and the world. This Element seeks to illuminate the ways in which the country and people form an integral part of the global capitalist system. This title is also available as Open Access on Cambridge Core.

Keywords: labour rights, digital surveillance, academic freedom, Xinjiang, Belt and Road Initiative

ISBNs: 9781108995566 (PB), 9781108999472 (OC)
ISSNs: 2632-7341 (online), 2632-7333 (print)

Contents

Introduction

Is China part of the world? Based on much of the political, media, and popular discourse in the West the answer is seemingly no. Even after four decades of integration into the global socio-economic system, becoming the 'world's factory' and second largest economy, most discussions of China continue to be underpinned and bounded by a core assumption – that the country represents a fundamentally different 'Other' that somehow exists apart from the 'real' world. Either implicitly or explicitly, China is often depicted as something that can be understood in isolation – an external force with the potential to impact the 'normal' functioning of things. This holds true for those who look at China from the outside and those who experience it from the inside, as 'Othered' representations of China are also common in Chinese official and unofficial discourses.

Both in China and the West – and across much of the Global South – this underlying assumption of China's inherent separation and difference, and its status as an external agent of change, cuts across political and ideological spectrums. It frames positive, negative, and ambivalent discussions about the country, particularly in relation to the increasing presence and entanglement of Chinese entities in the global socio-economic and geopolitical systems. Leaving aside the monumental question of Chinese exceptionalism as seen from within China, this Element focusses on heated international debates around some of the key issues of our present moment – that is, labour rights, digital surveillance, mass internment in Xinjiang, investment overseas, and the erosion of academic freedom. Through an examination of these five topics, we seek to recast the implicit core assumption of China as an external 'Other' that underpins so much analysis of contemporary China and provide a methodological roadmap for understanding China not as a discrete unit but as part and parcel of the contemporary global capitalist system.

Three Frames

So how is China 'Othered' and externalised in international political, media, and popular discourses and debates today? Three competing frames employed by ideologically distinct camps and with seemingly divergent analyses – but crucially rooted in the same core assumption of China as a separate 'Other' – currently hold sway. The first one is usually referred to as 'exceptionalism' but we would rather call it 'essentialism' to shift attention to how these discourses often put the emphasis on some innate 'essential' characteristics of 'China' and 'the Chinese'. In relation to Western debates, we use this term to refer to those perspectives that dismiss any attempt to find similarities between dynamics in

China and elsewhere. This form of argumentation tends to emphasise the set of attributes specific to a certain context as its defining elements, a line of reasoning reminiscent of the debates over China's 'national character' (国民性) that raged in China and the West a century ago and which remain eerily in vogue today – one just has to think about how Arthur H. Smith's infamous 1890 'treatise' *Chinese Characteristics*, a scathing racist indictment of China and its people once admired by revolutionary Chinese intellectuals such as Lu Xun, continues to be read today (even in China, where the book earns a surprisingly high score on the social media platform Douban). While in the past similar discussions revolved around issues of race, today's essentialist arguments mostly centre around the idea that authoritarian China cannot be compared with liberal democratic countries because they represent fundamentally different political systems – and any suggestion that there may be commonalities or overlaps is immediately and vociferously denounced as whataboutism and moral relativism.

Essentialism produces a myopic outlook and often manifests as self-righteous outrage at any suggestion that there might be more to the picture than what immediately meets the eye. From this perspective, there can be no linkages, seepages, or parallels between liberal democracies and authoritarian regimes. China must be analysed in isolation and any analysis must identify the authoritarianism of the Chinese Communist Party (CCP) as the only constant underpinning all problems. If outside actors are involved, such as foreign governments, multinational companies, or universities, their participation is perceived as the result of their corruption at the hands of the CCP rather than a reflection of wider systemic issues – hence, for instance, the widespread surprise when it was revealed that former US President Donald Trump expressed support for re-education camps in Xinjiang (Thomas, 2020). At their most extreme, these essentialising views insinuate that those seeking to identify convergences between China and elsewhere are apologists, useful idiots who unwittingly reproduce authoritarian talking points, or active agents undermining democracy in the service of authoritarian regimes.

The second approach is based on the age-old idea of 'changing' China. Its core assumption is that the more 'we' engage with China, the more the country is included in international systems and institutions, the more it will assimilate, which will hasten its inevitable transition to a free-market liberal democracy. We call it a 'maieutic' approach, in that it resembles the Socratic idea of dialogue as a way to challenge established ideas to lead to the refinement of the views and practices of an interlocutor. As such, it is an inherently moralistic view of China as an externalised 'Other' that is in need of reformation and integration.

This frame was perhaps dominant in the 1990s and 2000s, the golden age of neoliberalism and the 'end of history', but has been dealt a huge blow by the developments in Chinese domestic and foreign policy during the Xi Jinping administration (2013–). The crackdowns on Chinese human rights lawyers and activists linked to international civil society, the mass detention of Uyghurs and other ethnic minorities in Xinjiang, the repression of the Hong Kong movement, the rise of so-called 'wolf-warrior' diplomacy, and the willingness of the Chinese authorities to arbitrarily detain foreign citizens on spurious charges in order to use them as pawns on the international stage have undermined the argument that engagement will lead towards a more liberal democratic future for China.

As it has become more and more apparent that the likelihood of China transitioning into this perceived 'normal' member of the global community is low, some of those who previously subscribed to the maieutic approach have become disillusioned, adopting more essentialist views. This shift is generally expressed through a growing concern over how China is 'corroding' international institutions and norms and placing part of the blame on those actors (companies, universities, institutions, individuals) that are seen as complicit. In these cases, the moralism inherent in maieuticism is reconfigured and redirected – with China transitioning from the role of willing student to corrupting influence. But the inherent othering of the country remains intact.

The third frame – which we can term 'whataboutism' – refers to the dismissal of any criticism of China (and not only China) as hypocritical. An instance of this perspective could be seen in 2020 when, as protests against police brutality and racism erupted in American cities, social media platforms were awash with voices pointing out the hypocrisy of the US government in condemning the actions of the Chinese authorities in Hong Kong. Unable to control social unrest at home, what right do US politicians have to comment on what is going on in the former British colony? Similarly, in stigmatising the mass incarcerations of Uyghurs in Xinjiang, how could they ignore their own moral bankruptcy, made evident by the grim situation of the US prison system, the mass detention on the country's southern border, and the disasters unleashed by the global War on Terror? Conversely, how can anyone connected to the Chinese state (even loosely) dare to comment on the protests in the United States or the plight of immigrants in detention centres, considering the situations in Hong Kong and Xinjiang? These whataboutist arguments inherently frame what is happening in the United States (or any other Western country) and China as inherently separate and unconnected in any way – two sides of an equation that ultimately cancel each other out.

Whataboutism is such a common feature of the current debate that, in a recent op-ed, US-based Chinese human rights lawyer Teng Biao (2020) argued that constant comparisons between China and the United States have now become a 'virus' (病毒). Making a compelling case for how meaningless equivalencies have contributed to poisoning the debate, Teng highlights two types of questionable comparison: the first one is shallow congruences that do not extend beyond the surface level; the second is 'whataboutism' (比烂主义) proper. As Teng puts it: 'You say that corruption in China is serious, they say that the United States is the same; you say that China is culturally annihilating Uyghurs and Tibetans, they say that the United States also massacred the Native Americans and enslaved black people; you say China carries out extraterritorial kidnappings, they say that the United States attacked Iraq.'

While nothing prevents these criticisms levelled at China and the United States from being concurrently accurate – indeed, both are true but one does not excuse the other – Teng is correct in his grim assessment that the current China debate is mired in superficial comparisons, false equivalencies, and whataboutist argumentation. This is highly problematic for at least two reasons. First, whataboutism fosters apathy: if any form of criticism is just seen as hypocrisy, then what is the point of critical analysis? When does one become qualified to criticise? Second, it blinds by obscuring basic similarities and interconnections, muddying the waters and making it difficult to identify actual commonalities that extend beyond national borders and are inherent to the organisation of the global economy in our current stage of late capitalism. Whether whataboutism finds fertile ground simply owing to helpless narrow-mindedness or is an act of purposeful misrepresentation, the result is the same: whataboutist argumentation breeds myopic passivity, with the focus being placed on the detail rather than the broader picture. This not only makes meaningful discussion difficult but also impairs our ability to undertake effective political action.

Global China as Method

While the three frames outlined above are obviously ideal types, and in reality the boundaries between discourses are rarely that clear-cut, they generally coincide with starkly different political ideologies and thus come to divergent analyses of China. An essentialist framework is particularly common among those on the Right who perceive China as an existential (communist and authoritarian) threat to global capitalism and Western democracy that must be forcibly subordinated and integrated. Whataboutism is largely the domain of a growing segment of the Left, disillusioned with electoral defeats in liberal democracies (in particular, in the United States and United Kingdom), who are embracing romantic ideas of the People's Republic of China (PRC) as representing a form of 'actually existing socialism' with the potential to challenge global capitalism and legacies of imperialist colonial extraction. The maieutic framework is more common among liberal voices who see China as an authoritarian force – fundamentally distinct from, and incomparable to, Western democracies – that needs to be further engaged with and coaxed more fully into the institutionalised international order (including both 'free-market' global capitalism and global governance institutions) for it to become a 'normal' liberal democratic country.

Regardless of the different political stances, these views share one core assumption: that of China as an externalised, separate, and self-contained 'Other'. As we mentioned above, this premise serves to obscure rather than enlighten, and ultimately produces a distorted image of both China and the world. Still, it is important to acknowledge that all these frames contain within them elements of truth – which is part of the reason why they are attractive for so many. It is undeniable that China, just like any other place, has its own historical, social, cultural, economic, and political 'characteristics'. As such, understanding Chinese dynamics requires a certain level of particularism and any analysis that is not historicised and contextualised will unavoidably be superficial and misleading. At the same time, however, China is obviously part of the world and therefore shapes and is shaped by broader dynamics. Owing to this very embeddedness, there are valid debates to be had about ways of engaging with China that might help to put an end to certain abuses within the country, as well as Chinese participation in deleterious global trends.

The problem is that, if taken to the extreme and in isolation (as they often are), these positions lead to the toxic state of the discussion on China we are facing today, characterised by endless shouting, utter lack of communication, and a sense of despair due to the perception that we cannot even agree on the basic terms of the debate. Indeed, when we first tried to propose this argument, one of the criticisms we received was that there is no such a thing as a 'China debate' today: you either choose to stand up to the Chinese Party-State, or you are complicit in its atrocities (an assertion that is reversed in whataboutist discourse). In other words, the debate today is increasingly dominated by people demanding to know if you are with us or against us – a situation that is obviously incompatible with critical inquiry and understanding.

In this Element, we attempt to overcome the limitations of these frames by arguing that China does not exist in a vacuum or outside of the world. We follow Mizoguchi Yūzō's ([1989]2016) call to 'take China as method' by moving beyond an analysis of China that renders the country a flat caricature merely serving to reflect the ambitions and insecurities of those analysing it – a widespread phenomenon that he described as a 'reading of China without China'. In his words: 'A world that takes China as method would be a world in which China is a constitutive element' (p. 516). However, we propose taking this idea a step further. Rather than merely recognising China's existence as a component in the world in its own right, we highlight the importance of perceiving China as intimately entangled with global histories, processes, phenomena, and trends. In other words, China should not be seen as a discrete unit that can be understood in isolation. As such, we argue that understanding Chinese–global entanglements requires a fundamentally relational perspective, which moves away from a vision of the social world as comprised of static 'things' and conceptualises 'social reality instead in dynamic, continuous, and processual terms' (Emirbayer, 1997, p. 281).

In this way, this Element seeks to provide a framework for understanding the many manifestations of China in the world as resulting from material and discursive parallels and linkages, and embodying continuities and evolutions, as Chinese dynamics interact with and build on the historical legacies of the dynamic global capitalist system. Only by reconceptualising China as inextricably part of the world can we begin to understand what Chinese developments, both domestic and international, actually mean for people around the globe and present a more accurate depiction of the implications of China's rise on the global stage. In this, we aspire to follow in the footsteps of the late Arif Dirlik (2017, p. 1), who in his final book put forward two premises in which to anchor discussions of China today: first, the integration of the PRC into global capitalism over the last two decades requires criticism directed at it also to attend to the structure of the system of which it is a part; second, given the economic, sociopolitical, and cultural entanglements of global capitalism, criticism must account for outsiders' complicities – both materially and ideologically – in the PRC's failures as well as successes. While recent years have seen considerable debate over whether or not the Chinese socio-economic system operates according to the rules of capitalism, the point of this Element is not to argue for or against the idea that China should be narrowly defined as a capitalist country but rather to show how China is not an alternative to but rather an integral part of a global system that today works according to capitalist dynamics. If we do not identify and map these critical linkages and connections, our analysis will fail to illuminate and our criticism of, and struggles against, the overlapping forms of brutality characterising contemporary China and global capitalism will lose strength.

As such, we propose 'Global China' as an alternative analytical framework and methodological approach for discussing China today – that is, adopting a set of framings that interpret issues related to China's society and domestic and foreign policy in relation to broader trends and the underlying dynamics inherent to the stage of late capitalism we find ourselves in. While the idea of a 'global China' (lower case) is nothing new – one could easily argue that China has always been 'global', even at the height of the Mao era when the country was perceived as increasingly secluded from the rest of the world – here we refer to '*G*lobal China' (upper case) as a broader theoretical approach to the country, its position in the world, and its international engagements. In doing this, we draw from Ching Kwan Lee's ethnography of Chinese investment in Zambia, in which she argues for the need to '[push] the empirical boundary of China studies beyond China's territorial borders' (Lee, 2017, p. xiv). Lee has arguably done more than anyone else to give the concept of Global China a rigorous theoretical underpinning and popularise the term. In her words:

> China casts an outsize shadow on many different arenas of world development, challenging the field of China studies to abandon its methodological nationalism so as to catch up with China's transformation into a global force. Global China is taking myriad forms, ranging from foreign direct investment, labor export, and multilateral financial institutions for building cross-regional infrastructure to the globalization of Chinese civil society organizations, creation of global media networks, and global joint ventures in higher education, to name just a few examples. As many of these strands of outward development have originated from pressures and interests at home, the consequences of these external engagements are bound to have boomerang impacts on the home front, whether on regime stability, civil society growth, or national economic restructuring. Studying global China means reimagining China beyond China, connecting, contextualizing, and comparing 'Chinese' development with that in other parts of the world. (Lee, 2017, p. xiv)

In this way, Lee prompts us both to reorient our attention to China's global nature and to examine the implications of Chinese globalisation for domestic developments, thus connecting two domains that have largely been treated as separate. Our modest proposal is to expand this perspective by consciously and deliberately situating China globally, highlighting how issues that are often read as specifically 'Chinese' are in fact the result of complex dynamics and interlinkages that not only go beyond the Chinese borders but also necessitate a perspective that illuminates both China in the world and the world in China. As such, we follow in the footsteps of other scholars who have previously discussed issues related to the co-construction of 'China' as an imagined entity (see, for instance, Lee, 2018), have traced possible paths forward to go beyond the emphasis on the local that is typical of Area Studies (see, for example, the essays included in Nyíri and Breidenbach, 2013), or have pointed out the intricate entanglements and complex interdependencies between China and the global economy (Weber, 2020 and 2021), to argue that issues of Chinese domestic politics, economics, and social change should not be interpreted as separate from socio-economic and political developments globally. In our opinion, it is not enough to just say, as many have done, that Chinese domestic developments are now so consequential that they have important reverberations on the global stage – rather, domestic China should be read as an integral part of the broader global capitalist system and interpreted in this light. In other words, only by understanding China can one understand global capitalism and only by understanding global capitalism can one understand China – a fact which requires a significant conceptual and methodological reorientation.

Structure of the Element

This Element seeks to provide a roadmap for this reorientation by illuminating the ways in which the country and its people are intimately enmeshed in the global capitalist system. As we mentioned before, this is accomplished by examining the entanglements that characterise five key issues which frequently arise in current discussions about China: labour rights, digital surveillance and the social credit system, the mass detention of Uyghurs and other ethnic minorities in Xinjiang, the Belt and Road Initiative (BRI) and Chinese investment overseas, and academic freedom.

In the first section, we examine the issue of the Chinese labour regime since the country positioned itself as the new 'world factory' in the 1990s. The section challenges the competing narratives of those claiming that Chinese labour exploitation has prompted a global 'race to the bottom' and those who take the CCP's pro-labour rhetoric at face value, instead arguing that the configuration of Chinese labour has both shaped and been shaped by intensive engagement with global capitalism. In the second section, we examine Chinese surveillance technologies through the lens of the emerging social credit system, arguing that rather than representing a uniquely Chinese form of digital dystopianism, social credit is rooted in, and contributing to, a global trajectory of rapidly expanding algorithmic governance and surveillance capitalism. In the third section, we examine the mass detentions in Xinjiang, outlining the discursive and material linkages with the US-led War on Terror and the role of multinational corporations and educational institutions in facilitating these disturbing developments. In the fourth section, we turn to the BRI and overseas investment, looking at how Chinese initiatives often build on projects, ideas, and modes of operation put forward previously by Western actors and how new Chinese institutions can be seen as attempts to first emulate and then adapt established models. Finally, in the fifth section, we zoom in on academia, which has become a site of contention in debates over China's perceived influence abroad, outlining how the neoliberalisation of the university has opened up the possibility for outside actors (including Chinese ones) to threaten the fundamental principles of academic freedom.

It is our belief that, when discussing China, it is now more important than ever to strive to identify meaningful commonalities and interconnections underpinning dynamics at both discursive and material levels. If nothing else, that is where we can still hope to find some power to act. While the situations discussed in this Element present us with instances of entanglements that are frequently obscured in current debates on Chinese globalisation, these examples are also part of an extremely grim broader picture. Around the world we are seeing some seriously disturbing trends – a general authoritarian shift, the development of repressive technologies, and the further normalisation of mass detention regimes. As easy as it is to lay the blame for all this on China – and as undeniable as it is that Chinese actors are playing an important role in all this – these trends are not emanating solely from one country. Rather, the case of China is just one dramatic manifestation of interlinked, global phenomena – phenomena that are, in turn, shaped by broader forces. For this reason, we need to go beyond essentialist, whataboutist, and maieutic approaches and carefully document (and denounce) China's role in facilitating this dark turn, while also highlighting the ways in which Chinese developments link up with events elsewhere.

1 Chinese Labour in a Global Perspective

Labour has played an important role in defining China's global image over the past century. As early as 1919, the first conference of the International Labor Organization (ILO) recommended that the Chinese authorities adopt a social legislation, a request motivated more by the desire to protect Western workers from the 'unfair' competition from China's massive low-cost workforce than by genuine humanitarian concerns (Van Der Sprenkel, 1983). Although the internal strife of the Republican era, the Japanese invasion, and the autarchic policies of the Maoist era somewhat allayed these apprehensions, similar concerns re-emerged in force in the 1980s and 1990s, as China embarked on its path of economic reforms. It was then that the figure of the 'Chinese worker' made its way back to the international scene, through narratives that depicted them either as a victim of horrific exploitation or as a fearsome competitor who, with their willingness to work for next to nothing and accept any sort of abuse, was challenging the job security of their Western counterparts. In particular, it is often noted how China's economic growth in the reform era has been made possible by the exploitation of a vast surplus of rural workers freed by the land reforms of the late 1970s and early 1980s (Siu, 2020). As these workers migrated to urban centres and fuelled the booming private sector, their plight – long work hours, low wages, lack of access to essential public services due to the systemic discrimination of the household registration system, and awful workplace safety and health conditions – came to represent the flip side of the country's economic miracle, shaping China's negative reputation as a 'world factory' founded on the extraction of surplus value from an exploited workforce (Chan, 2001).

The plight of Chinese labour assumed even more global relevance as China entered the World Trade Organization in 2001. In the developed world, this event led to uncountable recriminations by trade unionists and policymakers about how China's 'social dumping' was undermining the well-being of workers in their countries; in the Global South, China was widely blamed for fuelling a 'race to the bottom' in labour standards, as governments chose to stay ahead of Chinese competition by promising prospective investors ever more favourable conditions (Chan, 2003). However, these perspectives do not always do justice to the complexity of the phenomena that were taking place at that time. On the one hand, they tend to overlook the fact that China inserted itself in an international context in which workers' rights and labour conditions were already being undermined by the global turn to neoliberalism and the collapse of the communist experiments. On the other, they often neglect to mention how, while China's entrance into the global capitalist system did indeed significantly change the dynamics of international competition with momentous implications for workers all over the world, China itself was forced to change and adapt in this process. It is this last aspect that this section examines, first by looking into the international pressures that the Chinese Party-State has had to face in its lawmaking efforts in the field of the labour law, then by highlighting the foreign connections of Chinese grass-roots labour organisations, and finally by discussing how some of the latest trends in labour activism in China should be read in a broader context of political desperation over the present and future of labour.

China's Labour Law

The narrative that portrays the Chinese authorities as wilfully suppressing the rights of its workers in order to gain competitive advantage in international markets has merit when it comes to the earliest stages of China's reforms, but if we take a closer look at the Party-State's policymaking efforts in the field of labour rights over the past two decades a more complex picture emerges. The most notable discovery is that – contrary to the popular discourse of the Chinese workplace as a ruthless arena where the law of the jungle prevails – the Chinese authorities have passed an impressive body of laws and regulations that address virtually every facet of labour relations. This regulatory effort has generally sought to parallel international practices in an attempt to bring the country in line with international standards and thus facilitate a smoother transition into the global capitalist economy. True, there are significant implementation problems: the regulations hardly keep pace with the structural changes in the economy (for instance, the emergence of the digital platform economy) and there is a fundamental imbalance between individual rights, which are regulated in detail, and collective rights, which are systematically watered down if not outright ignored (Chen, 2016). Still, these laws and regulations are far from inconsequential, especially considering the efforts that the Party-State and its organs have made to disseminate them among the public.

This turn to the law represents a conscious attempt by the Chinese authorities to overcome the language of class struggle and worker dominance that marked the Maoist era and promote a new rules-based order aimed at enticing foreign investors while also boosting the legitimacy of the Party-State (Gallagher, 2005, pp. 101–3). This shift has had mixed implications for Chinese workers. On the positive side, these regulations have provided workers with new tools to confront employers and local officials. On the negative side, this legislative activity has narrowed the possibilities for labour activism, both discursively and practically. From a discursive point of view, the dissemination of the labour law has established a new legalistic hegemony that has limited the imagination and repertoires of the workers, coaching them on which demands are permissible and which remain out of reach, in a dynamic not too dissimilar from the way in which labour movements in the West have been constrained through legal frameworks and the infusion of managerialism in labour relations throughout the neoliberal era (Hui, 2017; Gallagher, 2017). This can be seen, for instance, in the dominant pattern of industrial actions in China, which to this day remain atomised and focussed on demanding respect for *legal* rights, as well as in the fact that grass-roots organisations aiming to assist Chinese workers over the past two decades have focussed mostly on legal aid and dissemination (as we will see, the mid-2010s saw some experiments with collective bargaining among these organisations but they were quickly put to rest by the authorities) (Chan and Siu, 2012; Elfstrom, 2021; Friedman, 2014; Lee, 2007). From a practical point of view, these laws and regulations have managed to channel many workers' grievances through sanctioned channels, preventing (or at least delaying) them from escalating to more disruptive methods. This is apparent from the skyrocketing number of labour mediation and arbitration cases since the adoption of the Labour Law in 1994 – from 140,122 in 1996 to 2,119,000 in 2019, according to official data.

Does this mean that the Chinese labour law represents a conscious and successful 'soul-engineering' experiment by the Party-State on the Chinese working class? Yes and no. There is no doubt that every piece of labour legislation passed in China over the past decades has been the subject of careful consideration by Chinese policymakers. Although the debate generally has revolved around technical issues and the suitability of the said set of rules to the country's economy in its current stage of development, concerns about how the new laws would impact labour activism were always very present. Scholars have also extensively studied how China's labour law and legal system have affected the subjectivities of Chinese workers. For instance, in describing the Chinese labour law as a massive hegemonic experiment (in the Gramscian sense) undertaken by the Chinese Party-State in its turn to capitalism, Elaine Sio-Ieng Hui (2017) has offered a categorisation of Chinese workers in accordance with their interiorisation of this new legalistic discourse. In her ethnographic research conducted at the turn of the millennium, Ching Kwan Lee (2007) has shown how Chinese migrant workers are more likely to resort to a legalistic repertoire and go through official channels in their protests, compared with the overtly political language and disruptive methods adopted by older laid-off workers in the state industry. By focussing on Chinese workers' experiences of the legal system, Mary Gallagher (2007) has documented how Chinese workers often get 'disenchanted' and radicalised when they face the inefficiencies and inequalities of this system. In the same vein, we have argued that most workers who go through their lives without direct involvement in a dispute are more likely to live in a condition of 'misinformed enchantment', that is, have a very vague idea of the specific provisions of the law but believe that, should they get involved in a labour dispute, the legal system will come to their succour (Franceschini, 2016, p. 153). Still, what often goes unnoticed in these debates is how, in writing and enacting these laws, the Chinese authorities did not have free rein but had to mediate between the interests of different actors, both domestic and international. It is in these policymaking dynamics that we see how the issue of labour rights in China is truly global.

The Case of the Labour Contract Law

The long and troubled process that led to the passing of China's Labour Contract Law (LCL) in 2007 provides a perfect case in point to highlight the global relevance of labour rights in China. For years, the new law – the most significant piece of labour legislation in China since the passing of the Labour Law in 1994 – had been debated behind closed doors in Chinese academic and policymaking circles. Two positions had come to dominate the discussion: one that advocated for more government control and intervention in industrial relations to guarantee workers' rights and another that argued for better enforcement of existing laws (Gallagher and Dong, 2011). In March 2006, the Chinese authorities finally published a draft of the law that strongly leaned towards the former position and asked the public for its feedback. The response was overwhelming, with over 192,000 comments submitted in one month, 65 per cent of them allegedly coming from 'ordinary workers' mobilised by the lowest rungs of the Chinese official trade union (Guan, 2007).

Foreign chambers of commerce in China were also active participants in the process and their involvement was one of the aspects of this story that attracted the most attention, both in China and abroad. In particular, the American Chamber of Commerce in Shanghai (AmCham), the US-China Business Council (USBC), and the European Union Chamber of Commerce (EUCham) all submitted comments that were very critical of the draft law. Besides a series of technical points, these documents emphasised that the LCL was going to undermine the attractiveness of the Chinese market in the eyes of foreign investors. The greatest concern was that the LCL would lead to a rise in labour costs. As the then President of the EUCham bluntly remarked to a journalist from the *South China Morning Post* on 26 April 2006: '[T]he strict regulations of the draft new law will limit employers' flexibility and will finally result in an increase of production costs in China. An increase of production costs will force foreign companies to reconsider new investment or continuing with their activities in China' (Shi, 2006). Another argument was that it was pointless to enact new regulations when the existing laws were not properly implemented. According to the comments submitted by AmCham in March 2006:

> It shall be noted that the most significant problem existing in labor issues in PRC is not the lack of protection of laborers by labor laws and regulations, but the fact that the laws are not fully observed. ... Solving these long outstanding problems shall mainly depend on establishing perfect law enforcement procedures, strengthening law enforcement and putting into effect existing provisions, but not proposing unduly high requirements in addition to existing liabilities of enterprises and destroying existing legal order. Otherwise the abnormal situation that 'the one who violates laws remains unpunished while the one who observes laws is punished' must be deteriorating. (AmCham Shanghai, 2006, pp. 20–1)

Finally, the law was deemed not appropriate given the current stage of Chinese economic development. As an AmCham representative wrote to the Standing Committee of the National People's Congress in April 2006:

China is still a developing country and its main focus at this stage is still economic development, as correctly pointed out by Premier Wen Jiabao. In making and revising laws, the starting point should be the specific circumstances of China, not good intentions, and hastily-set goals ... In the highly competitive global economy of today, the welfare of Chinese workers depends not only on protections afforded by labour law, but also depends on the survival and steady growth of the enterprises in which they work. It is not wise to kill the chicken to get the egg. (Cited in Gallagher and Dong, 2011, pp. 47–8)

Facing this kind of pushback from both foreign and domestic companies, the Chinese authorities substantially revised the draft. This is particularly evident if we consider the provisions concerning the trade union (Franceschini, 2009). The draft of March 2006 included at least two provisions which would have strengthened the role of company unions in their dealings with the employers: the first provided that company policies and internal regulations which directly affected the interests of the employees had to be discussed with and approved by the union; the second mandated that, when a labour contract could not be fulfilled owing to dramatic changes in the objective circumstances on which the labour contract was based and it was necessary to lay off more than fifty employees, the employer had to explain the situation to the company union or all the staff, reaching a consensus before carrying out the lay-off plans. Even though grass-roots unions in China are structurally so weak that even with these new prerogatives they would hardly have posed a threat to managerial authority, both provisions were drastically revised. Not only was the union's right of veto on the internal regulations expunged but the final draft also stated that a company should ask the opinion of the union only on the matter of lay-offs involving at least twenty workers or more than 10 per cent of the workforce. In the same fashion, other articles on delicate matters, such as permanent contracts, non-compete agreements, and the signing of labour contracts, were substantially revised to accommodate the point of view expressed by the business community.

Without delving into the issues surrounding the implementation of the LCL – which was first undercut by the onset of the global financial crisis and then rendered outdated by structural changes in China's labour market (Gallagher et al., 2015; Gallagher, 2022) – the same tension between different interest groups became apparent on several other occasions. At the national level, in July 2012 the Chinese authorities published a draft amendment of the LCL focussed on dispatch labour, which in one month drew 557,243 comments from the public (Geng and Zhou, 2012). In October, Chinese media reported on pressures coming from Chinese state-owned enterprises, invested in maintaining an unregulated labour dispatch system, so it came as a surprise when the amendment was actually passed at the end of the year (Jiang, 2012). At the local level, in 2010 local authorities in the Guangdong Province attempted to rein in a wave of labour activism by pushing forward new rules that, if adopted, would have significantly empowered workers to bargain collectively with their employer (Chan, 2014, p. 704; Hui and Chan, 2016). As the Guangdong authorities discussed a revision of the provincial Regulations on the Democratic Management of the Companies that would have laid the foundations for genuine collective wage bargaining, the Shenzhen authorities decided to accelerate the legislative process of a city regulation on collective negotiations. It was expected that both regulations would be passed quickly but in a matter of weeks they disappeared from the political agenda. According to scholars and labour activists, this turnaround was due to pressure coming from the entrepreneurial community in Hong Kong, which had immense economic interests in Guangdong and had made its displeasure publicly known by acquiring pages in the media of the former British colony in which they expressed their critical views (*China Labour Bulletin*, 2014; Hui and Chan, 2016).

There is an argument to be had about how much clout these entrepreneurial complaints carried in shaping the ultimate decisions of the Chinese authorities. However, these examples are significant for at least two reasons. First, they make it clear that, while the Party-State has ultimate authority in shaping policy in this field, all these laws and regulations are the result of complex negotiations and represent a balancing act between the agendas of different constituencies, including global business. Second, they turn the narrative of Chinese labour forcing a global race to the bottom on its head, as we witness global capital itself exerting pressure on China to keep down its labour standards.

Globalised Activism

Another important encounter between Chinese labour and the world took place at the grass-roots, in the realm of labour activism. To this day, only one trade union is legally allowed to exist in China, the All-China Federation of Trade Unions (ACFTU 中华全国总工会), a mass organisation structured along Leninist lines that is supposed to act as a 'transmission belt' between the working class and the Party-State (Harper, 1969). Although on paper it has around 300 million members, because of its structural subservience to both managers and officials the ACFTU is notorious for its inability to represent the interests of its constituency, leaving a gap for worker representation. As throughout the 1980s the reforms started eroding the welfare and job security of state workers and migration from the countryside scaled up rapidly, discontent simmered, until in 1989 workers turned out en masse to join the student-led pro-democracy protests and establish their own independent unions (Zhang, 2022). The ensuing repression disproportionately targeted workers and, with a few very minor exceptions, in the following years labour activism was on the ebb (Lin, 2022).

The situation began to change in the mid-1990s and it is at this historical juncture that we begin to see the global connections inherent in Chinese labour activism. Two events stand out in this regard. First, in 1993, a fire broke out in a small Hong Kong-owned toy factory in Shenzhen, claiming the lives of eighty-seven migrant workers, mostly young women (Chan A., 2022). Labour non-governmental organisations (NGOs) in Hong Kong publicised the tragic incident and an effective international campaign was launched that linked the big-brand toy companies in the developed world to the exploitation that went on inside their supplier factories in Asia. This not only resulted in the international toy industry recognising a code of conduct drawn up by the Hong Kong labour NGOs but also led to increased international scrutiny of labour conditions in Chinese factories at both the local and the international levels. Second, the decision of the Chinese authorities to host the United Nations Fourth World Conference on Women in Beijing in 1995 signalled the beginning of a new stage for the development of Chinese civil society, including a new type of NGO focussed on labour issues (Howell, 2022).

While the first labour NGOs had a strong focus on gender issues, the late 1990s saw the emergence of organisations that focussed on the plight of migrant workers more generally. This cohort further grew in the late 2000s, under the administration of Hu Jintao and Wen Jiabao, taking advantage of the political openings offered by the Party-State's newly minted discourse of social harmony. These organisations had strong ties to international civil society and, indeed, drew most of their funding from international donors, a fact that was apparent if one considered their geographical concentration in Beijing, with its large number of embassies and international foundations, and Guangdong Province, next to Hong Kong and its vibrant civil society. Given the intrinsic sensitivity of labour issues, these labour NGOs were rarely allowed to register as non-profit entities and usually ended up with a commercial registration or no registration at all, which made them vulnerable to crackdowns by the authorities, which came periodically (Franceschini and Nesossi, 2018). They mostly engaged in four kinds of activities: the establishment of workers' centres, where they organised educational classes and recreational activities; dissemination of information on labour rights; social surveys and policy advocacy; and provision of legal consultation and, in some cases, representation (Chan, 2013; Xu, 2013). Significantly, in all these activities, these organisations carefully sought to reproduce the notoriously individualistic language of the *legal* rights of the Party-State, a decision made out of necessity that gained them considerable criticism, in particular from scholars who argued that this strategy had the adverse effect of undermining worker solidarity (Lee and Shen, 2011).

In the early 2010s, a few labour NGOs started going beyond this legalistic approach to advocate for collective bargaining (集体谈判) as a new strategy to protect workers' broader interests (Chen and Yang, 2017; Froissart, 2018; Franceschini and Lin, 2019). These organisations began openly intervening in collective disputes, training workers on how to choose their own representatives to confront the employers, an important step forward towards the empowerment of China's working class. Until then, collective bargaining had remained the domain of the ACFTU, which had watered it down to 'collective negotiation' (集体协商), a largely formalistic method of bargaining that was entirely handled by the official union under the assumption that employers and employees shared identical interests. Significantly, even in this case, the shift was supported by global civil society, in particular the China Labour Bulletin, a prominent labour NGO based in Hong Kong (Froissart, 2018). When the Chinese authorities clamped down on these organisations at the end of 2015 (and then over and over again in the following years), they took care to emphasise the foreign connections of these activists, resorting to the state media to run a smear campaign centred on the alleged embezzlement of money coming illegally from abroad and links to 'hostile foreign forces' hellbent on fostering chaos in the country (Franceschini and Nesossi, 2018).

The crackdown on labour NGOs took place within the context of a broader attack by the Party-State against local NGOs and individual activists engaged in politically sensitive fields, most of whom received financial support from abroad and had strong connections with international civil society. A fundamental step in this sense was the passing, in April 2016, of a Law on the Management of Foreign NGOs' Activities within Mainland China aimed, among other things, at curtailing access to foreign funding by these organisations and individuals (Franceschini and Nesossi, 2016). What we have witnessed over the past few years is a systematic attempt by the Party-State to 'cleanse' Chinese civil society by severing its international ties, which in itself is a testament to the global nature of these organisations (Snape, 2021). However, it is also important to note how China is not alone in this rejection of the global when it comes to civil society. We are witnessing similar dynamics not only in several authoritarian or semi-authoritarian countries where the spectre of 'coloured revolutions' is regularly used as a straw man to justify periodical crackdowns and more restrictive laws on civil society but also – perhaps more worryingly – in many liberal democracies, where fears of societal infiltration and co-optation by agents of hostile foreign forces are becoming increasingly pervasive. As local and international NGOs scramble to adapt to the changing circumstances and navigate the political restraints imposed by both donors and the governments of the countries they operate in, the future of global civil society appears more uncertain than ever.

Dark Forebodings

The aspects discussed in this section obviously do not exhaust all global linkages of Chinese labour. Much could be written about China's technical co-operation with the ILO, about how labour rights have been used as a diplomatic tool (for instance, most recently by the European Union, which demanded that China commit to ratifying ILO conventions against forced labour in order to move forward with a landmark investment deal), about the various corporate social responsibility initiatives that transnational corporations push on their Chinese suppliers, and about how rising labour costs in China are now leading to a drastic reconfiguration of supply chains in labour-intensive industries. All of this, however, points to a single fact: issues related to labour rights and industrial relations in today's China are deeply intertwined with the global capitalist system. It is not only about China proactively driving down labour standards globally through a 'race to the bottom' but also about China adapting to global capitalism, giving in to international pressures, and conforming to broader trends, all while trying to create a labour regime that allows the country to accumulate the most capital from integration into global markets.

Long gone are the days when China presented an alternative occupational model through its 'work unit' (单位) system and the 'iron rice bowl' (铁饭碗) of lifetime employment. As Joel Andreas (2019, pp. 8–9) has pointed out, Maoist China stood out among all the variations of the twentieth-century communist project for offering its urban citizens employment that was perhaps more permanent than in any other country and for turning workplaces into sites of governance of primary importance. Four decades of economic reforms have seen the unravelling of this model. From the first experiments with Special Economic Zones in the late 1970s to the mass migrations of rural workers to the cities starting in the 1980s, from the introduction of labour contracts in 1986 to the wave of lay-offs of state workers of the 1990s, the legacies of the Maoist labour policies have been systematically dismantled. Basic social security policies followed only later, as an afterthought when the social consequences of this transition were becoming unmanageable and threatened the stability of the whole system. At the same time, the political discourse of the workers as 'masters' of the state and the enterprise has been replaced by the anodyne and technical language of 'legal rights', with the implications described above. The result is that today, although the CCP still claims to represent 'the vanguard of the Chinese working class' and China's constitution still extols the virtues of labour, secure employment has become a myth for the vast majority of the country's workforce. Extreme precarity has become the norm, just like in the rest of the world.

From the revolutionary promise of lifetime employment, China is now at the forefront of the neoliberal dream of atomised labour, in which the worker is reduced to a simple *homo economicus*. This can be seen most prominently in two regards. First, as we mentioned above, the Chinese trade union is powerless owing to its structural limitations; at the same time, the Party-State, assisted by the union, has been clamping down hard on any form of labour activism that poses even the most basic threat to its monopoly over labour representation, be that labour NGOs experimenting with collective bargaining or individual activists attempting to boost workers' solidarity. While the Chinese case is indeed extreme, this is just a manifestation of another global trend that began in the 1980s – that of the bureaucratisation of the trade unions and the undermining of the collective power of the workers. Second, China is a pioneer when it comes to the 'new economies'. According to ILO estimates, in 2019 China had only about 6.23 million workers directly employed in the digital platform economy, less than 8 per cent of the nearly 80 million that constitute the workforce in the sector (Zhou, 2020). According to other accounts, China's digital economy employs as many as 180 million people, or nearly one-quarter of the total Chinese workforce (Chen et al., 2020). As the Chinese Party-State struggles to revise its regulatory apparatus to protect them (Gallagher, 2022), it is these workers – whether delivery workers subject to impossible work rhythms or employees in high-tech companies pressured into working impossible hours – who now most often appear in the local and international news owing to their dreadful labour conditions, just like their counterparts in other parts of the world do.

One decade ago, it was the Taiwanese Foxconn, an electronics contract manufacturer that produces gadgets for some of the main international brands (most famously Apple), which came to represent the worst excesses of exploitation in the Chinese workplace. In 2010, when the company employed about one million workers in China, Chinese and international media widely reported on a series of attempted suicides among its ranks, eighteen in that year alone (fourteen of whom then died) – all young migrant workers aged between seventeen and twenty-five – and exposed the alienating circumstances in which these youths had to toil (Chan J., 2022). Today, the spotlight is on new professional figures: delivery workers and white-collar employees in high-tech companies. The difference between the workers who made the news yesterday and those who do today is that, although Foxconn did not spare any effort when it came to breaking down any potential for solidarity among its employees, at the end of the day Foxconn workers still lived and toiled in shared facilities, so at least had a chance to exchange experiences, discuss their plight, and nurture a sense of belonging to a group. Workers in the platform digital economies most often lack even this. Not only are they atomised owing to the very structure of the sectors they operate in but the Party-State is making sure that they remain that way by detaining those very few activists who attempt to boost a sense of class solidarity, such as Chen Guojiang, a delivery worker detained in Beijing in early 2021 and then charged with the catch-all crime of 'picking quarrels and making trouble' for his activities aimed at exposing the malfeasances of companies and providing support to his fellow workers (Feng, 2021).

In such a context, it is with considerable scepticism that, in 2021, we read news reports about Chinese youths choosing to 'lie flat' (躺平), that is, to resort to passive resistance or outright opt out of the rat race that is the neoliberal workplace of today (Chen, 2021; Day, 2021). While commentators are eager to see in this the sign of yet another impending 'awakening' of Chinese workers – in this case, mostly white-collars, one decade after another much-discussed alleged 'awakening' of which second-generation migrant workers were the protagonists – we see in it evidence of a defeat. It is when everything else fails, when there are no venues for organising collectively, when there is no political imagination left, that one chooses to 'lie flat' or resort to other forms of weapons of the weak. And the fact that in these phenomena many see a promising sign really says much about the predicament of labour in the brave new world heralded by these new economies, not only in China. Sadly, in the neoliberal world of today, the bar for labour activism has now been set so low that even 'lying flat' has become a revolutionary act. Instead of looking at these situations pertaining to labour rights and worker resistance as an exclusively 'Chinese' phenomenon, it is these types of connections and dialectic interactions between local dynamics and global trends that we should really be investigating when discussing the plight of Chinese workers.

2 Digital Dystopias

The proliferation of atomised platform labour in China overlaps with other worrying developments in the digital sphere, both in China and elsewhere. In recent years, as it has become increasingly clear that the Internet and information and communication technologies (ICTs) have largely failed to live up to their promise of being 'liberation technologies' ushering in a new era of freedom, enlightenment, and democracy, the spectre of the emergence of dark forms of high-tech surveillance and social control has dominated depictions of advances in digital technologies. From facial recognition to 5G, China has been at the centre of the global imaginary of this malevolent technological turn, with the country being depicted as a site of uniquely authoritarian technological development and also a ground zero from which oppressive technologies will emerge before being exported (along with China's authoritarian model) around the world. In the words of the social theorist Benjamin Bratton (2021, p. 54): 'In the West, China is now so deeply associated with technology that *anxieties about technology are projected into anxieties about China*, and to an extent vice versa.'

The depiction of China as the locus of the perversion of the digital sphere into a corrupting, illiberal force pervades political, media, and popular discourses in the West and reaches its zenith around discussions of the country's ambition to develop a 'social credit system' to monitor the socio-economic activity of citizens, businesses, and organisations. One only needs to turn to publications like *The Economist*, which has run with headlines like 'China Invents the Digital Totalitarian State' (*Economist*, 2016a), or the tweets of characters like Donald Trump Jr, who has claimed that vaccine passports in the USA are a 'Chinese-styled social credit system' pushed by 'authoritarian leftists' (Villarreal, 2021), to get a sense of the existential dread surrounding the idea of Chinese-driven digital innovations that have the potential both to surveil and restrict the individual's involvement in the social and economic realms. As such, social credit embodies deeper fears surrounding China's emergence on the global stage, paired with imagined visions of the country upending the status quo socio-economic order in the West and 'infecting' Western societies with its corrupting authoritarian modes of digital existence.

In this way, social credit has come to signify the onset of a dystopian future that is being seeded in the authoritarian and illiberal context of contemporary China but which will fan out across the globe, reformulating the relationship between individuals, corporations, and states and recoding our expectations for private life. But how unique to China's authoritarian model is this attempt to leverage new technologies and big/alternative forms of data in order to more easily categorise, monitor, standardise, and ultimately quantify socio-economic activity and moral behaviour? This section seeks to answer this question by situating the Chinese social credit system in a broader context, outlining the ways in which the discourses and practices of social credit both parallel and build on attempts around the globe to assess economic risk, regulate economic activity, and socially engineer capitalist notions of 'creditworthiness' into society.

Making Credit Social

So what is social credit and how is it linked to emerging forms of data-driven governance? In Western discourse it is frequently depicted monolithically, as an all-encompassing, technologically sophisticated, big-data-driven rating apparatus where people receive scores based on their social and economic activities that then facilitate or limit their socio-economic participation (Carney, 2018). When comparisons are made, it is often likened to an episode of the dystopian sci-fi show *Black Mirror* and/or is depicted as an extension of some traditional Chineseness – either a new manifestation of Confucian ethics or the realisation of the goals of Mao-era surveillance (Clover, 2016; Palin, 2018; Zeng, 2018). As such, social credit is depicted as a dark digital perversion that is able to emerge in the particular authoritarian context of contemporary China – a place characterised in orientalist terms as both having a uniquely totalitarian history and being at the forefront of the development of new digital technologies. In the words of *The Economist*:

> In the West, too, the puffs of data that people leave behind them as they go about their lives are being vacuumed up by companies such as Google and Facebook. Those with access to these data will know more about people than people know about themselves. But you can be fairly sure that the West will have rules – especially where the state is involved. In China, by contrast, the monitoring could result in a digital dystopia. (*Economist*, 2016b)

This form of essentialist argumentation has the potential to be convincing because it contains a kernel of truth: there are fewer impediments to the creation of a big/alternative-data-driven mass surveillance regime in China than in the West. However, it also sets up a false binary between the West and China that can cause us to miss the crucial ways in which particular practices in China are both shaped by and contribute to shaping global processes and tendencies that transcend states or political systems. In other words, it obscures the parallels and linkages, as well as the ways in which Chinese experiments with social credit build on and evolve out of established modes of assessing socio-economic risk and engineering economic moralities, that are crucial for understanding the dynamics of Chinese social credit and its implications for people both inside and outside of China.

In order to really come to grips with the full ramifications of Chinese social credit, it is necessary to move beyond a singular focus on authoritarian social control. While Chinese policymakers undeniably see social credit as a tool for surveilling the population, this is far from the only ambition for the system. Social credit can be seen as an outgrowth of Chinese experiments with integrating excluded and marginalised populations (particularly in rural areas) into the formal socio-economic system. Throughout the 1990s and 2000s, a number of microcredit and financial inclusion initiatives were initiated by the Chinese government, often inspired by or in conjunction with international financial institutions and the global microfinance movement. For instance, the China Association of Microfinance – an institution aiming to support the establishment of microcredit programmes and promoting inclusive finance – was established in the Chinese Academy of Social Sciences with support from CitiBank and other international financial institutions (Loubere, 2019). However, despite these attempts at integrating excluded individuals, groups, and areas into the formal economy, lending bottlenecks persisted at least in part due to a lack of credit information for risk assessment. As such, there have been discussions about streamlining the monitoring of the economic activity of citizens, businesses, and organisations in China in order to improve and monitor the functioning of the economic system going back to the beginning of the century (Zhang, 2020). These discussions took a much more concrete form in 2014, with the publication of a notice from the State Council outlining plans to build a nationwide social credit system by 2020. This high-level policy document outlined steps that should be taken in order to create a system that collects credit records and information for all citizens while also promoting a culture of trustworthiness. The ultimate aim is for the system to facilitate commercial activity and promote socio-economic development (State Council, 2014).

Despite the goal of having an integrated, nationwide system by 2020, social credit is still not fully unified or centralised. Like most policy frameworks in China, the social credit system is being subjected to the country's distinctive policy modelling process, where local governments produce their own interpretations of policies, which then vie to become national models (Heilmann, 2008). As Zhang Chenchen has pointed out, the ongoing construction of social credit includes 'an extremely diverse range of decentralized, experimental, and fragmented programs across social, economic, and legal fields' (Zhang, 2020, p. 566). By 2019, approximately twenty-eight localities were labelled official 'demonstration cities' and allowed to experiment and innovate within the limitations of the policy framework (Daum, 2019). A novel aspect of social credit, however, was that eight large internet companies were also initially given licences to run their own pilots (Loubere, 2017). The most widely discussed private social credit system (often conflated with social credit more broadly by those outside China) is Alibaba's Sesame Credit, which utilises opaque algorithms to arrive at social credit scores for their customers. Those with high scores have been able to access a range of benefits from other Alibaba businesses and their partners (Bislev, 2017). However, while Sesame Credit is significant because of the huge amounts of economic data held by Alibaba through Alipay and Ant Financial, the Chinese government ultimately cancelled its pilot status along with the other private companies, and these initiatives now 'essentially function like loyalty rewards programs' (Matsakis, 2019). In recent years, different aspects of the social credit system have increasingly come into focus, particularly with regard to which entities will collect and report which types of data, but the system nevertheless remains in flux and in development.[1]

Based on the above, Chinese social credit should be understood as an evolving policy framework with a number of facets – all of which are under-pinned, but not solely defined, by modes of surveillance. For one, social credit is envisioned as an administrative enforcement mechanism, which will utilise data analytics to ensure regulatory compliance through rewards for companies and organisations that consistently comply with regulations and various blacklists and other forms of punishment for violators (Daum, 2019; Zhang, 2020). This component of social credit reflects the wider global expansion of data-driven, algorithmic governance techniques, and to fully understand the dynamics at play it is necessary to highlight commonalities and divergences between China's social credit system and emerging regulatory regimes around the world (Backer, 2018). At the same time, social credit is a response to the fact that China lacks the infrastructure to systematically assess and evaluate eco-nomic risk for individuals, businesses, and organisations (Daum, 2017), which adds costs to commercial activity and has created a situation where there is a perceived general lack of 'trustworthiness' in society that is holding back socio-economic development. As such, Chinese social credit should be under-stood as an attempt to build a comprehensive economic risk assessment system (which draws on data from the social realm) allowing for smoother economic integration, increased participation in the formal economy, and a form of moral social engineering aimed at creating a trustworthy (or creditworthy) citizenry.

Social Credit as a Credit System

While the predominant depiction of social credit is as an exoticised, novel, dystopian practice, it is more accurate (albeit more boring) to take credit rating/ scoring systems as our initial point of comparison and analysis. As mentioned above, China's lack of a uniform credit rating infrastructure has proved difficult for financial institutions and has resulted in high transaction costs and lending bottlenecks. The social credit system seeks to fix this problem by helping financial institutions assess risk, essentially greasing the wheels of Chinese capitalism. The difference between social credit and traditional credit scoring

---

[1] For up-to-date analysis and translations of key developments in the social credit system, see the website China Law Translate https://www.chinalawtranslate.com/.

systems elsewhere (which generally base scores on economic factors alone) is that the Chinese version proposes to draw on larger amounts and alternative types of data from both the social and economic spheres. However, this is a difference in degree, rather than of fundamental nature. As such, we can gain important insights into the potential functioning of social credit in China by looking at the practices and outcomes of credit scoring in other contexts, and by examining Chinese social credit we can anticipate the ways in which credit scoring systems elsewhere might expand their risk assessment criteria in the age of big and alternative data.

Indeed, if one bothers to look, it quickly becomes apparent that Chinese ambitions to leverage different forms of data from the social realm for assessing economic risk are not unique at all. For example, the San Francisco-based company Affirm, which was founded by PayPal's Max Levchin, scrutinises the digital footprints of potential customers to make lending decisions (Reisinger, 2015). And more cases can be found among an emerging class of digital lenders across the Global South that are 'innovating' new methods for assessing risk, often using methods such as psychometric tests in order to 'judge the character' of potential borrowers (*Economist*, 2016c; Loubere and Brehm, 2018).

The financial technology (fintech) company LenddoEFL provides a glimpse into how the global digital finance sector envisions data collection, personal privacy, and the future of credit scoring. Lenddo began as a digital lending company and was one of the first to lend through the Facebook platform. However, the company quickly moved out of the lending business and into providing credit rating and identity verification services based on big/alternative data analysis to other lenders. In 2017 Lenddo merged with the Entrepreneurial Finance Lab (EFL) – founded at Harvard – which utilises psychometric testing and other forms of data collection to create credit scores. LenddoEFL uses a huge amount of private personal data from their customers to assess risk, including information about contacts, social media activity, messaging and emails, browsing history, and user location, to name just a few. Moreover, their collection of data extends beyond their own customers and to their contacts, with these interactions feeding into the risk assessment. Jeff Stewart, the founder and CEO of Lenddo, has described the company's 'innovative' use of data by saying: 'I think that what we'll see in the data and as society evolves ... [is that] who you hang out with and how you interact with them is going to be part of how you're judged'. He has also articulated a vision of future credit scoring based partially on a customer's social connections, with those having 'high-quality' friends receiving a higher score (Privacy International, 2018).

If these words had come from a Chinese official rather than the CEO of a major fintech company, we could be relatively sure that there would be a flurry of mainstream media activity clearly highlighting the dystopic implications, replete with references to *Black Mirror*. However, if we turn again to *The Economist*, we find that in contrast to their fears surrounding China's 'digital totalitarianism', the magazine writes glowingly of the potential of psychometrics and alternative data collection utilised by EFL and other fintech providers in their quest to 'financially include' the Global South. While Chinese social credit is presented as an existential threat, fintech surveillance capitalism is seen to be ushering in a non-threatening future 'in which lending is almost entirely digitised, combining psychometrics with social media and mobile phone records ... Lenders, looking for an edge, will find ever more ways to peer into their customers' souls' (*Economist*, 2016c). The point here is not to highlight the double standards of *The Economist* but rather to illuminate the ways in which the practical aspects of the collection and analysis of big/alternative data that underpins Chinese planning around social credit parallel developments in the broader fintech sector and the evolution of digital financial capitalism globally.

Social Credit as Social Engineering

Part and parcel of the quest to draw on alternative forms of personal data to assess risk and create a credit rating system is the aim to socially engineer new forms of socio-economic relations into the population based on capitalist notions of 'creditworthiness' and participation in the formal market. In the case of the Chinese social credit system, there is an explicit ambition to facilitate market participation by increasing 'trustworthiness' (守信) and 'integrity' (诚信) through moral education as part of a wider civilisational imperative (Daum, 2019). While this civilising component of social credit is rooted in long-standing Chinese state goals of creating a 'modern' citizenry, it also draws on global discourses associated with good governance, socio-economic development, and economic participation. In particular, the moral and developmental language of social credit parallels much of the discourse utilised by microcredit and financial inclusion programmes that aim to transform 'underdeveloped' places and people into developed subjects through integration into the market. For microcredit and financial inclusion proponents like Muhammad Yunus (the Nobel Peace Prize-winning founder of the Grameen Bank), inclusion into the market is actually a matter of life and (developmental) death. In his words: 'Financial services are like oxygen. We need to breathe, without it we collapse. The absence of financial oxygen makes people collapse, makes people dysfunction ... The moment they are connected to financial services, they become active' (Arns, 2018).

Echoing the psychometric turn discussed above, Chinese social credit also resonates with the idea pushed by behavioural economists – and promoted by the World Bank – that good economic decision-making and behaviour can be instilled through 'tweaks' and 'nudges' targeting individuals, ultimately resulting in broad social benefits (World Bank, 2015). These ideas have been popularised in recent decades, culminating in the 2017 Nobel Prize in Economics being awarded to Richard Thaler for his work on 'nudge theory' and the 2019 Nobel Prize in Economics being awarded to three development economists who pioneered the randomised control trial (RCT) for socio-economic development. Both of these approaches have been key to the expansion of social experiments on populations (mainly in the Global South) in an attempt to socially engineer different types of behaviour (Chelwa and Muller, 2019). These behaviouralist and experimentalist approaches see individual poverty and broader patterns of underdevelopment as being partly the result of difficulties surrounding making decisions under conditions of pervasive distrust. From this perspective, one of the solutions to underdevelopment is the creation of trusting societies, as highlighted in the World Bank's *World Development Report 2015: Mind, Society, and Behavior*: 'Social preferences and social influences can lead societies into self-reinforcing collective patterns of behavior. In many cases, these patterns are highly desirable, representing patterns of trust and shared values' (World Bank, 2015, p. 9). The parallels with the Chinese government's ambitions for social credit to 'build an environment of trust' (General Office of the State Council, 2016) are obvious.

Credit and Surveillance Old and New

As legal scholar Jeremy Daum points out: 'There can be great comparative value for democracies in watching China's integration of technology, governance, and society, but meaningful comparison requires accurate understanding' (Daum, 2019). Taking this one step further, accurate understanding cannot be rooted only in detailed comparisons of technology, governance, and surveillance capitalism in separate contexts, but rather must be based on analysis of parallels, divergences, overlaps, and entanglements globally. As such, it is necessary to be able to identify crucial commonalities with what is happening in China and elsewhere and how these things are connected both materially and discursively. If we fail to do this, then we either ignore one of the most important developments in digital social control because we relativise through whataboutist arguments (i.e. everyone is doing it so who cares);

adopt an essentialist stance and assume that emerging forms of dystopian digital surveillance, such as social credit, are something unique to China's brand of authoritarianism; or perceive Chinese digital experiments as a corruption of the liberatory teachings of digital technologies, without recognising that what is happening in China is actually the logical continuation (and intensification) of phenomena elsewhere – and in this sense China has been an exemplary, not subversive, student in the classroom of global capitalism. In short, any of these approaches makes it impossible to see how developments in China are actually rooted in, and contributing to, a global trajectory of rapidly expanding alternative data analytics, algorithmic governance, and surveillance capitalism.

As such, rather than seeing technology itself as something neutral that can be turned to good or evil depending on which actor is utilising it, we should perceive these forms of high-tech surveillance capitalism as emerging through, and facilitating the ambitions of, the global capitalist system and its participants. Dreams of fully integrating populations into the formal economy allowing for 'frictionless' commercial activity, as well as the transformation of individuals into both market consumers and producers of market-relevant consumption data, are ultimately dreams moulded by capitalism.

They are also nothing new. The functioning of debt in capitalist societies has always been underpinned by technologies of surveillance of both individuals and their social networks. Traditional credit scores have sought to surveil economic activity in order to judge if someone is creditworthy, and those without a sufficient paper trail (i.e. not sufficiently surveillable) need to turn to family or friends who can act as guarantors and be subjected to surveillance themselves (Loubere, 2021). The ability to leverage digital technologies to collect huge amounts of different types of data, along with the algorithmic automation of data analysis, represents the next logical step in the evolution of capitalist credit rating systems and the wider goal of expanding economic integration. Chinese social credit certainly represents an important example of this development, alongside others around the world. The fact that China is not unique does not render these developments any less dystopian, but rather more so. As we continue to see the inevitable sharpening of repressive tools of surveillance and socio-economic control wielded by the rich and powerful in ways that will only entrench and exacerbate the inequalities and forms of subjugation inherent to the capitalist political economy, it becomes more important to clearly illuminate the shared rationalities, practices, and potential outcomes of these systems, as the failure to do so will doom our chances of collectively militating against them and reorienting these technologies towards the creation of more just societies.

3 Xinjiang

Another example of dynamics in China that require us to identify global linkages can be found in the 're-education' camps of Xinjiang, which have become a major focal point of international tensions in recent years. These camps constitute a fundamental part of the 'People's War on Terror' initiated by the Chinese authorities in response to a rise in violent attacks carried out by Uyghur civilians against Han civilians in late 2013 and 2014 (for a detailed timeline of these events, see the appendix to Byler et al., 2022). While initially it was only religious leaders who were sent to the camps, by 2017, after Xinjiang came under the administration of hard-line governor Chen Quanguo, the Party-State began assessing the whole Muslim population in the region for signs of 'extremism', which often meant simply practising their religion in any visible form. Since then, Uyghur, Kazakh, and other peoples have been increasingly prevented from practising their traditional ways of life, and their mosques and other sacred places demolished or transformed (Thum, 2020). Not only have hundreds of thousands of people – and this is a conservative estimate – been detained in prisons and 're-education' camps but many of their relatives have been assigned to work in factories far from their homes and their children placed in residential boarding schools where they receive 'patriotic', non-religious education. These camps also do not exist in a void but have deep historical roots and significant global connections. It is to these roots and connections that we turn in this section.

Historical Precedents

Scholars have pointed out how the current situation in Xinjiang is rooted in long-standing Han suppression of Uyghur identity, as well as in discourses of 'blood lineage' and 'thought reform' emerging in the Maoist era (Cheek, 2019; Cliff, 2016; Yi, 2019). However, what is unfolding in Xinjiang can also be considered an extension of settler colonial logics and practices dating back to European colonialism, where native populations were brutally suppressed and concentrated on reservations (Nemser, 2017). For instance, the recent revelations that the Chinese government is engaging in the forced sterilisation of Uyghurs echo the eugenics campaigns targeting native populations in the United States and elsewhere in the twentieth century (Amy and Rowlands, 2018). Similarly, the dispossession and relocation of Kazakh and other nomadic-pastoralist communities in Xinjiang to make space for state-led enclosures of Kazakh grasslands for ecotourism purposes find echoes in green colonial land grabs that have taken place across the world – from the establishment of the national parks in the United States through the dispossession and genocide of Indigenous people, to the less bloody development of wind farms within reindeer herding lands in Norway (Salimjan, 2022).

More specifically, the Xinjiang camps as carceral infrastructure aimed at reinforcing a colonial presence represent the culmination of a century-long global process in which concentration camps were first conceived by the Spanish in Cuba in the late 1890s, expanded by the British in South Africa during the Boer War, normalised by all warring factions during the First World War, and finally manifested in the extreme variants of the Soviet Gulag and the Nazi Lager, before lapsing into the more familiar forms of 'black' detention sites that became common in Latin America in the 1970s. In this regard, proponents of whataboutist arguments relentlessly point out how Western liberal democracies have also repeatedly established concentration camps in recent history. And they are not wrong. As Tzvetan Todorov (1986, pp. viii–ix) wrote in his preface to Primo Levi's *The Drowned and the Saved*:

> illegitimate (if not 'useless') violence [such as that of the concentration camps] is not a prerogative only of nazi and communist regimes, it can also be encountered in the authoritarian states of the third world and even in parliamentary democracies. It is only needed that the voices of the political leaders present it as necessary, even as urgent; immediately it will be raised by ubiquitous media and soon thereafter supported by the court of authors and intellectuals who know well how to come up with rational justifications for the choices of those in power: these choices are always made in the name of the 'defence of democracy' or the 'lesser evil'.

From the British experience in Malaysia and Kenya in the 1950s – stories that the British government has consistently attempted to hide and manipulate (Monbiot, 2020) – to the latest experiments of the US government with extra-judicial detentions in Guantánamo Bay and the mass internment of undocumented immigrants, examples abound.

And there is another unsettling historical lesson that should be considered. As journalist Andrea Pitzer (2018, p. 13) has argued, concentration camps are deeply rooted in modernity, particularly in advances in public health, census taking, and bureaucratic efficiency that took place in the late nineteenth century. They are also inextricably linked to inventions like barbed wire and automatic weapons. At the same time, 'only rarely have governments publicly acknowledged the use of camps as deliberate punishment, more often promoting them as part of a civilizing mission to uplift supposedly inferior cultures and races' (Pitzer, 2018, p. 6). In this sense, the Chinese authorities are not only maintaining this tradition by maximising the 'benefits' of the latest progress in surveillance technology to establish its twenty-first-century version of concentration camps in Xinjiang, but they are also lifting heavily from established discourses to justify such an endeavour. From this point of view, it is possible to argue that while the Xinjiang camps are eerily similar to their predecessors in terms of power dynamics and discursive justifications – which makes the testimonies from the Nazi camps or the Soviet Gulag particularly poignant when read in light of what is happening in Xinjiang today (see, for instance, the discussion of the work of Primo Levi in relation to Xinjiang in Franceschini and Byler, 2021) – they are also distinct in that their operation is shaped by the latest technological advancements.

Discursive Links

Concentration camps in Xinjiang are not monads even in the context of today's world. On the contrary, it is possible to identify both discursive and material linkages between the events unfolding in northwest China and global trends. On the discursive side, the Chinese authorities have widely appropriated international discourses of anti-terrorism related to the US-led War on Terror to justify their securitisation of Xinjiang (Roberts, 2020). David Brophy (2019) has written about the 'war of words' over the Xinjiang question between Chinese authorities and foreign critics, pointing out how Chinese officials justify the camps by citing what they see as a worldwide consensus – which emerged in the wake of the global War on Terror – on the need to combat radicalisation through pre-emptive measures that identify, isolate, and rehabilitate potential extremists. According to the logic of the Chinese authorities, if the camps in Xinjiang go beyond any Western attempt at countering extremism, it is simply because counter-extremism policing in the West, focussing only on select individuals, has not done enough to prevent acts of terrorism.

In the same vein, Darren Byler (2019b) has put on display the poignant similarities between the attempts to construct a 'human terrain system' through weaponised ethnography by the US forces in Iraq and Afghanistan and the way in which the Chinese authorities are acting in Xinjiang, while also unearthing how shifts in US military doctrine in the field of counter-insurgency since the late 2000s were first received and adapted in China before being put into practice in Xinjiang. This link is also made in a recent influential, and controversial, paper by Sheena Greitens, Myunghee Lee, and Emir Yazici (2020), in which the authors argue that China's rhetoric about Central Asia's Uyghur diaspora began to shift following the attacks of 11 September 2001, with the Party-State drawing connections between Uyghur organisations and jihadist groups, especially those in Afghanistan and Pakistan, instead of emphasising pan-Turkic separatism.

It is also possible to find less explored but no less poignant assonances between discourses adopted by the Chinese authorities in Xinjiang and those pushed by some governments in the West in relation to their minority, immigrant, and refugee populations. One such example is the language of 'gratitude'. As Christian Sorace (2021) has highlighted, the Party-State in Xinjiang is enacting 'gratitude education campaigns' as a direct instrument of control within the re-education camps, where, to prove that they are rehabilitated, detainees must convincingly demonstrate their absolute loyalty and gratitude to China, the Communist Party, and Xi Jinping himself. Besides testimonies of 'graduates' from the camp presented by Chinese state media, Sorace quotes a campaign launched in early 2017 in Ürümqi under the name of 'three gratitudes, three wishes' – that is, 'gratitude to General Party Secretary Xi Jinping', 'gratitude to the Communist Party, 'gratitude to the mighty motherland', 'wishing General Party Secretary a healthy life', 'wishing the mighty motherland glory and prosperity', and 'wishing for ethnic harmony'.

Although such ritualised incantations and repetitions are the legacy of a sort of campaign politics that has been perfected by the CCP over the century of its existence, in a separate essay Sorace (2020) points out how such demands for gratitude are not uncommon even in the West. As examples, he quotes former President Donald Trump's delay in approving COVID-19 relief cheques because he insisted that his signature be on them, as well as George W. Bush complaining in 2007 that the Iraqis whose lives he destroyed did not feel sufficiently grateful. This echoes Mimi T. Nguyen's (2012) research, which has shown how, after being granted citizenship in the United States, refugees from areas devastated by US imperialism are expected to show 'gratitude' for the 'gift of freedom'. According to Sorace (2020, p. 168), 'these hysterical demands reveal the insecurity of sovereign power' and are aimed at maintaining a status quo that the authorities perceive as precarious, in China and beyond.

Material Connections

The implications of this co-optation of counter-insurgency discourses emanating from the War on Terror by the Chinese authorities remain highly controversial in that taking the 'anti-terrorism' rhetoric at face value risks legitimating the policies of the Party-State in Xinjiang (Robertson, 2020). However, the material side of the global dimension of the camps presents us with a more straightforward example of the 'complicities' existing between Western capitalism and the People's Republic of China (Dirlik, 2017). Indeed, while the dominant narratives about the camps revolve around essentialist authoritarian or even totalitarian frames, there are good reasons to present a critique of the camps framed in terms of their embeddedness in the global capitalist system, if not as an extreme manifestation of a new form of capitalism itself. For instance, in light of the fact that the camps system is enforced through a comprehensive infrastructure of biometric surveillance and physical checkpoints, as well as an army of police contractors, Darren Byler (2022b, p. xiii) has argued that camps are a symptom of 'terror capitalism', which he defines as 'a distinct configuration of state capital, techno-political surveillance, and unfree labor, [which] might begin with targeted groups like the Uyghurs, but . . . might also find similar expression among Muslim populations in Kashmir or with watch-listed Latinx asylum seekers in Texas'.

'Terror capitalism' – or whatever we call this new facet of capitalism – is global in nature. There is no denying that both Chinese and multinational corporations are deeply involved in the development of surveillance technologies that are used in Xinjiang. As Darren Byler (2020) has highlighted, local authorities in Xinjiang have recently started outsourcing their policing responsibilities to private and state-owned technology companies in order to enhance their surveillance capacities through private–public partnerships. These companies, especially those that are leading the way in the field of artificial intelligence, operate well beyond Chinese borders. In an uncanny instance that he cites, in April 2020 Amazon received a shipment of 1,500 heat-sensing camera systems to take the temperatures of its workers during the coronavirus pandemic. These units came from Dahua, a Chinese company that in 2017 received over 900 million USD to build comprehensive surveillance systems to support the expansion of extra-legal internment, checkpoints, and ideological training in Xinjiang (Hu and Dastin, 2020).

As documented by Gerald Roche (2019), the situation in Xinjiang has also involved the global mercenary industry. In January 2019, the Frontier Services Group (FSG), a private security firm spearheaded and led by Blackwater founder Erik Prince from 2014 until April 2021, announced plans to open a 'training centre' in Xinjiang (Shepherd, 2019). The company was established by Erik Prince with investment from Citic Group, one of China's largest central state-owned investment companies, as a publicly traded aviation and logistics firm specialising in shipping in Africa and elsewhere, as well as conducting high-risk evacuations from conflict zones, declaredly with a particular focus on helping Chinese businesses to work safely in Africa (Cole and Scahill, 2016). FSG first announced plans to open an office in Xinjiang in March 2017 (Fan, 2017) and a few months later it appointed Lü Chaohai as head of its northwestern regional operations (Bloomberg, 2019; FSG, 2017). Previously, Lü was the vice-president of the Xinjiang Construction and Production Corps, also known as *bingtuan*, the paramilitary-commercial organisation that has been tasked by the CCP with the development of Xinjiang's economy since the 1950s. Although all the information about the company's involvement in Xinjiang has since been taken offline (Ordonez, 2019), the announcement highlighted another problematic set of complicities between global capitalism and repressive practices of cultural suppression in China and beyond.

At the same time, foreign universities are actively taking part in developing the technology and techniques that the Chinese authorities are using to ramp up surveillance in Xinjiang. Leading international academic institutions, including the Massachusetts Institute of Technology, have come under scrutiny for having research partnerships with artificial intelligence companies that have business ties with state security organs in the region (Harney, 2019). To cite just a few specific examples, in August 2018 Anil K. Jain, head of Michigan State University's Biometrics Research Group, travelled to Xinjiang's capital, Ürümqi, and gave a speech about facial recognition at the Chinese Conference on Biometrics Recognition, for which he also sat on the advisory board (Rollet, 2019). In 2019, the University of Technology Sydney (UTS) and Curtin University in Perth both had to review their links to Chinese companies and researchers over concerns that the partnerships could be helping China persecute Uyghurs (McNeill et al., 2019). UTS, in particular, was revealed to have a 10 million AUD partnership with CETC, a Chinese state-owned military tech company that developed an app used by Chinese security forces to track and detain Uyghurs. Finally, also in 2019, it emerged that to bolster their DNA tracking capabilities, scientists affiliated with China's police force drew on material and expertise provided by Kenneth Kidd, a prominent Yale University geneticist, while using equipment made by Thermo Fisher, a Massachusetts company (Wee, 2019). Over the past couple of years, academic journals have had to retract articles for ethical violations related to the informed consent procedures followed by the authors in collecting DNA samples from Uyghurs and other ethnic minorities in northwest China, while several more cases are still under investigation (Marcus, 2020; Wee, 2021).

In fact, there are many instances of Chinese companies approaching foreign universities, either directly or through their shadow subsidiaries, and offering funds under the generic banner of 'supporting collaboration between academia and industry'. While fostering international partnerships and collaboration is undoubtedly part of the core mission of universities, as James Darrowby (2019) has pointed out, the key areas for proposed collaboration in the case of Chinese companies often focus on the development of the next generation of audio-visual tracking tools, which represent significant potential for military and domestic surveillance applications. With neoliberal universities often forced to seek and accept funds from any available source to justify their very existence in the eyes of the government, they frequently sidestep due-diligence procedures and end up abetting projects that contribute to ramped-up surveillance and repression in China and elsewhere. And this kind of complicity does not even touch upon matters such as the nature of research affiliations with foreign institutions, conflicts of interest, undisclosed double appointments, and the dissemination and application of sensitive project outputs. Essentialist depictions of this situation are widespread but again only provide us with a partial picture. While emphasis is frequently placed on the nefarious activities undertaken by Chinese state actors aimed at corrupting Western higher education institutions, there is much less attention paid to the ways in which the marketised and managerialised university has become eminently pliable to outside interests through funding and research partnerships, a topic which we will return to in more detail in Section 5.

It would be a mistake, however, to reduce corporate involvement in Xinjiang to high-tech actors involved in surveillance and carceral capitalism, as the camps also represent an opportunity for more 'traditional' business. As Darren Byler (2019a) has shown, since 2017 Chinese factories have been flocking to Xinjiang to take advantage of the cheap labour and subsidies offered by the re-education camp system, a move that can partly be explained by the rising labour costs in more developed parts of the country. Significantly, even before the beginning of the camps, the Chinese Party-State was already planning to move more than one million textile and garment industry jobs to the region (Patton, 2016). And these domestic companies are not the only ones benefiting from the ramped-up securitisation of the area. Far from producing exclusively for domestic consumption, forced Uyghur labour feeds directly into the supply chains of at least eighty-three well-known global brands in the technology, clothing, and automotive sectors, including Apple, BMW, Gap, Huawei, Nike, Samsung, Sony, and Volkswagen (Xu et al., 2020). This connection has become so notorious that in October 2020 concerted pressure from trade unions and advocacy groups led ethical trade associations such as the Better Cotton Initiative (BCI) to announce that they would no longer work in Xinjiang (BCI 2020), while several affiliated brands declared they would no longer source cotton from Xinjiang or work with suppliers who employed labour from Xinjiang.

In that 'the goal of the internment factories is to turn Kazakhs and Uyghurs into a docile yet productive lumpen class – one without the social welfare afforded the rights-bearing working class' (Byler, 2019a), the camps in Xinjiang appear to be a manifestation of a capitalist system always hunting for new workers and markets to exploit in order to sustain itself. In other words, it could be argued that the camps are not really an anomaly, nor are they a sign of the capitalist system being corrupted by China, but simply a feature of the system itself. These systemic features can also be seen, for instance, in the policing and incarceration systems of the United States, where widespread racial profiling leads to the detention of a hugely disproportionate number of young black men – a demographic that is systematically maintained and reproduced as a low-wage labour supply (Benns, 2015). In fact, if we consider the discursive and material linkages and parallels outlined above as a whole, the Uyghur Human Rights Policy Act as passed by the US legislature in 2020 and the blacklisting of a few Chinese companies working on artificial intelligence and facial recognition, while highly symbolic and undoubtedly important, play little more than a cosmetic role rather than addressing the root causes of the abuses.

The Limitations of the Debate

In such a context, both whataboutist and essentialist arguments, while constructed in opposition to each other, serve to obscure the situation in Xinjiang in similar ways – by fragmenting and atomising our analysis and thus causing us to miss crucial parallels, linkages, and complicities. Whataboutism does this dismissively, resorting to moral relativism and claims of hypocrisy to rationalise away wrongdoing while failing to recognise that global practices are connected. Essentialism does it by attributing the horrifying situation in Xinjiang solely to the CCP, thus failing to identify the linkages emerging from the global system. As such, both whataboutism and essentialism serve as blinders, forcing us to focus on a single part of the picture while ignoring the bigger story. These atomised and myopic perspectives fail to provide us with the analytical tools necessary to diagnose and organise against the horrors unfolding in Xinjiang and elsewhere.

Instead, frames such as Darren Byler's (2022b) 'terror capitalism' are better suited to capture the situation in Xinjiang, in that they focus on both the atrocities taking place in the region and the global connections underpinning these dynamics. By perceiving the Xinjiang camps as a result of processes of state power being channelled through private and public infrastructure and institutions to intensify ethno-racialisation and produce a contemporary colonial system of exploitation and dispossession at a frontier of global capitalism, we are better equipped to understand what is happening in northwestern China today and to attempt to organise against the processes that are the root cause of the crisis. This perspective also increases our grasp of the manifold socio-economic implications of the rapid development of surveillance and other groundbreaking technologies of control in China and beyond.

4 Belts and Roads

Recently, a friend who works in an NGO was interviewed by a journalist. After discussing the risks and challenges involved in Chinese coal projects in a certain country, the friend explained that, despite the local authorities' supposed commitment to working towards a coal-free future, a handful of these projects were still moving ahead. At that point, the journalist asked, 'Are any of these projects part of the Belt and Road Initiative (BRI)?', to which the friend pointedly retorted, 'Does it really matter, since they are all moving forward?'

This anecdote illustrates not only how today's international discussions about China's global engagements have come to be predominantly framed in terms of the BRI but also that problems that extend far beyond the nationality of the actors involved – such as coal and the environmental catastrophe that we are all facing – are reduced to petty politics and perceived through the lens of national units rather than at the system level. To paraphrase our friend's retort: does it really matter whether the coal plants are part of the BRI (whatever that might mean) when they should not exist regardless? Whether the investors behind them are Chinese, Australian, or European? Shouldn't we instead focus on addressing the root causes of the problems at stake, which in this specific case is the persistence of an economic system that still heavily relies on, and continues to incentivise, fossil-fuelled power despite all the evidence that this is leading to disaster?

Much of the discussion surrounding the BRI in recent years has had the consequence of obfuscating broad common challenges that we are facing in our current iteration of global capitalist development – from eroding labour rights to massive indebtedness, from widespread dispossession to environmental degradation. The framing of the BRI as a massive scheme by the Chinese Party-State to subvert democratic institutions in some settings, reinforce authoritarian tendencies in others, and enhance China's overall political and economic influence abroad has prompted endless discussions about the challenges posed by Chinese actors abroad. Because of this renewed focus on Chinese overseas activities, broader issues related to the very functioning of capitalism have been relegated to the background. Yes, there is no denying that massive influxes of investment and aid from China have buttressed authoritarian governments, that loans from China have contributed to huge debt in certain countries, and that Chinese projects all over the world have led to labour exploitation and environmental damage. Yet, by focussing our attention exclusively on the BRI we often miss how these dynamics are rooted in broader, long-term domestic (both in China and in the host countries) and international trends that have much deeper roots than the ephemeral phenomena that we see today. Similarly, by putting the emphasis exclusively on the negative impacts of China's international engagements, we risk overlooking how these problems are situated within the broader picture of global capitalism. This, in turn, not only leads us to adopt an exceedingly essentialist view of China in relation to its international activities but also causes us to lose sight of the biggest questions of our age. To avoid this pitfall, we suggest that an accurate analysis of China's international role today cannot focus on China in isolation but rather needs to identify the ways in which Chinese overseas engagements parallel, link up with, and build on local and global capitalist dynamics.

One, No One, and One Hundred Thousand BRIs

Where does this obsession with the BRI come from? If we look back at the recent history of Chinese engagements abroad, it becomes clear that the level of contentiousness that we witness today is nothing new. Already in the 1950s, the Chinese authorities played a fundamental role in the creation of the non-aligned movement and began sending technicians and workers abroad to provide assistance to other developing countries in what would later come to be known as the Global South (Sorace and Zhu, 2022). In the 1960s, in the wake of the Sino-Soviet split and at the height of the Cold War, the Chinese leadership committed to waging Third World struggle against the twin imperialisms of the United States and the Soviet Union, a position known as 'Third-Worldism' (Bräutigam, 2009, p. 37; Galway, 2022; Teng, 2019). Although in later decades, as the Cold War wound down and China embarked on its path of economic reform, the Chinese Party-State set aside the anti-colonial project underpinning this rhetoric, China's global role continued to be at the centre of heated debates. The 1990s saw Chinese companies beginning to 'go out', but the real turning point for China's international engagement came in the late 1990s and early 2000s, as Beijing officially announced the 'China Goes Global' strategy and concurrently joined the World Trade Organization (Hong and Sun, 2006; Ye, 2020, chapter 4). If, on the one hand, this landmark event fostered liberal hopes for the country's supposed democratic future, on the other it led to widespread concern about how China's compressed labour costs might affect other economies (Solinger, 2009).

However, over the last decade, as the Chinese government, companies, and organisations have become increasingly assertive on the global stage, the imaginaries of the potential of the BRI to alter the existing order have intensified the alarm about China's global rise. Xi Jinping first announced the BRI during state visits to Kazakhstan and Indonesia in late 2013, but the Initiative gradually took shape over the following months and years. Although international attention usually focusses exclusively on its infrastructural component, according to the official action plan released in March 2015, the BRI rests on five pillars – policy coordination, facilities connectivity, unimpeded trade, financial integration, and people-to-people contacts – all of which should be considered equally important (Xinhua, 2017; Garlick, 2019; Zhang, 2021b). Soon, wild figures began circulating, the most widely cited one being the estimate that BRI investment would add over one trillion USD of outward funding for foreign infrastructure in the decade starting from 2017 (OECD 2018, p. 3). Such ambitiousness rattled nerves in Western policy circles. Some scholars have since highlighted how the BRI is in many regards chaotic and very far from being a masterplan for world dominance envisaged by the Chinese authorities (Jones and Zeng, 2019; Ye, 2019); others have pointed out that, despite the apparent chaos, particular mechanisms in China's governance system have enabled Chinese policymakers to coordinate different actors in pursuit of China's core national interests in its international interactions (Zhang, 2021b: chapter 3). This general uncertainty about what the BRI is and how it works has had the effect of rekindling old Cold War fears about China's global rise and influence.

Boosted by propaganda efforts from the Chinese authorities and an equally robust critical response, the debate has become extremely polarised. On one extreme are those who see the BRI as a benign plan under the aegis of South–South co-operation, which will boost infrastructure in countries that could not otherwise afford it, thus reviving their ailing economies; on the other are those who argue that development aid and foreign investment are ultimately a Trojan horse through which the Chinese authorities aim to extract much-needed resources, appropriate strategic assets, and boost their political influence worldwide. This, combined with the fact that today Chinese actors are more eager than ever to associate themselves with the BRI for purposes that range from economic gain to political legitimacy, has led to the disproportionate focus on the Initiative as a frame to understand China's global engagements mentioned above. This, in turn, has produced a number of cognitive biases.

Confusion and Cognitive Biases

First, by employing the BRI as a frame to analyse China's international engagements, we end up neglecting other significant manifestations of the phenomenon that we refer to as 'global China' (lower case, as opposed to the 'Global China' of the theoretical approach that we outlined in the introduction). As Ching Kwan Lee (2017, p. xiv) has argued: 'Global China is taking myriad forms, ranging from foreign direct investment, labor export, and multilateral

financial institutions for building cross-regional infrastructure to the globalization of Chinese civil society organizations, creation of global media networks,
and global joint ventures in higher education, to name just a few examples.' As
such, by restricting our focus to the BRI we end up overlooking many important
aspects of contemporary Chinese globalisation. In particular, the BRI lens tends
to orient us towards the large and formal aspects of global China, implicitly or
explicitly producing an image of the Chinese state as a monolithic actor pushing
forward a coherent, top-down global strategy. What is missed in this depiction
of China's global engagements are the multitude of small- and medium-scale,
informal, and often (semi-)illicit forms of Chinese investment and interaction
overseas. From the political upheaval and environmental ramifications produced by the sudden irregular migration of tens of thousands of Chinese alluvial
gold miners to Ghana (Loubere et al., 2019), to the struggles and negotiations
between Chinese petty entrepreneurs and a variety of local actors in diverse
contexts around the world (Xiao, 2015), 'bottom-up global China' is arguably
just as important for understanding contemporary Chinese globalisation as
anything associated with the BRI but has only received a fraction of the
attention.

At the same time, since there is a substantial lack of clarity about the nature of
the BRI – no official list of BRI-related projects exists, nor are there stringent
criteria for a project to qualify for the BRI label – there are instances of some
grass-roots or 'bottom-up' engagements being depicted or even marketed as part
of the BRI, even though they have no connection whatsoever to the Party-State
and are certainly not part of Chinese development planning. This compounds the
confusion and strengthens the impression that the Chinese authorities have a hand
in nearly everything that involves Chinese actors abroad. In other words, fragmented and chaotic 'bottom-up global China' sometimes gets recast as part of the
monolithic centralised vision in ways that at best mislead and at worst completely
distort. For instance, in a recent case that attracted considerable negative media
attention, a Chinese fugitive with a Cambodian passport named She Zhijiang
established a partnership with a local warlord to turn the latter's headquarters in
Shwe Kokko village, in Myanmar's Kayin State, into a 'smart new city' osten-
sibly catering to the development of the IT industry, but actually a safe haven for
online gambling and fraud operators (Cheng, 2021). She Zhijiang engaged in
a high-profile public relations campaign to fashion himself as a successful
patriotic member of the Chinese business community overseas and his project
as an important component of the BRI in the region, only to have the Chinese
Embassy in Myanmar publicly disavow the project – although this did not do
much to persuade many external observers, who, to this day, still refer to Shwe
Kokko as a 'BRI project'.

Cases like these remind us that global China is far more than the BRI alone and should be understood not only through the geopolitical and economic frames that dominate the current debate but also in broader terms that consider the extreme variety of Chinese international engagements and without losing sight of how these are connected to domestic actors and dynamics both in China and abroad. At the same time, the BRI itself should not be understood as a monolithic and coherent strategy by the Chinese state. Rather, the Initiative and everything within its orbit should be perceived through the lens of domestic Chinese policy formulation and implementation, which is characterised by high levels of vagueness, fragmentation, and experimentation at the local level (Heilmann, 2008; Mertha, 2009). In this sense, the BRI parallels the ways in which domestic central development frameworks – such as the Open Up the West Programme (西部大开发) and the Construction of a New Socialist Countryside (建设社会主义新农村) – come to be embedded in local contexts and utilised by diverse local actors to push forward agendas and projects pre-dating the policy itself and reflecting local and often personal – rather than central – priorities (Loughlin and Grimsditch, 2021).

Second, many of the current analyses that focus on the BRI tend to put too much emphasis on what is observable at this moment, neglecting the history and background of what we are witnessing today. A solid understanding of China's politics, society, and foreign policy in historical perspective should be a prerequisite for any analysis of global China's contemporary emergence. For instance, one cannot discuss China's engagements in Southeast Asia without referring to how the BRI has integrated with the Greater Mekong Subregion programme, a minilateral regulatory dialogue comprising the five Mekong states – Cambodia, Laos, Myanmar, Vietnam, and Thailand – and China's Yunnan province and Guangxi autonomous region that began in the 1990s (Raymond, 2021). Nor should one overlook how today's cultural diplomacy and people-to-people initiatives discursively build upon China's legacy of 'Third-Worldism' and engagement with the Global South since the middle of the last century (Galway, 2021). Indeed, by neglecting how certain dynamics that we witness today have their roots in China's not-so-distant Maoist past – as well as longer-term histories of Chinese overseas migration and diaspora communities – we risk missing important insights. Hong Zhang (2020 and 2021a) provides a fitting example of this in documenting how China's international construction and engineering contractors (ICECs) are born of aid-delivering entities that initially were administered by China's ministries and subnational governments in the pre-reform era. Stripped of their governmental status and incorporated into firms in the 1980s and 1990s, today China's ICECs play a fundamental role in determining the agenda of the Chinese authorities when it comes to their 'development finance'.

Third, and most importantly, by focussing our analytical gaze on the BRI, we miss how Chinese actors overseas are, like anyone else, embroiled in the specific circumstances of the host country as well as the dynamics of global capitalism and are therefore subject to similar rules of the game as their Western counterparts, with all the implications this entails. This can be seen, for instance, in the structure and functioning of the multilateral financial institutions whose establishment was promoted by the Chinese authorities in recent years, in particular the Asia Infrastructure Investment Bank (AIIB), which is often seen as an instrument to promote China's geopolitical interests. There is no doubt that the AIIB represents a clear attempt by China to play a more influential role in the area of global multilateral finance. It was proposed by China, is headquartered in Beijing, and China holds by far the largest number of shares and voting rights. However, rather than overturning the existing model used by established multilateral development banks, the AIIB has emulated the models of other banks – although in a much more stripped down and 'lean' manner. It has also recruited numerous veterans from the World Bank, Asian Development Bank, and other international financial institutions, and to date has over 100 members. The AIIB is explicitly mentioned in official BRI documents but in terms of enhancing China's role in 'financial integration' (National Development and Reform Commission et al., 2017). As can be seen in the first few years of operation, around half of the Bank's projects were co-financed with Bretton Woods banks, and the top recipient of AIIB loans has been India, which views the BRI with significant suspicion (Inclusive Development International, 2020).

Even one of the cases that are most often cited as proof that China is resorting to 'debt trap' diplomacy – that of the Hambantota Port in Sri Lanka – is, in fact, an apt example of how taking Chinese loan (mis)practices out of context can be severely misleading (for a detailed discussion of the case, see People's Map of Global China, 2021). Rather than being seen as a case of nefarious Chinese plotting to take over strategic foreign assets, the Sri Lankan government's decision in 2017 to enter into a public–private partnership with China Merchants Group (CMG) and transfer 80 per cent of the shares of the port to the company is actually the result of multiple forms of indebtedness (and the different strings that come attached) to a variety of international actors. On the one hand, the port project was conceptualised as being a joint venture between Sri Lanka and a private company and was primarily financed through both commercial and concessional loans from the Export–Import Bank of China. So certainly there was plenty of Chinese debt, as well as an understanding of

Chinese commercial actors being involved. But the reason for the terms of the port project being renegotiated and the shares going to CMG is an economic downturn forcing Sri Lanka to turn to the IMF for an emergency bailout. The IMF's terms (as they often are) were that non-strategic public assets would be privatised and the proceeds used to service debt obligations. It is in this context, under duress and being pressured into quick action by the IMF, that Sri Lanka made the decision to transfer the majority of the port to CMG. As such, the Hambantota Port incident is less a story of Chinese debt trap diplomacy and more a story of Chinese actors wading into a complex local environment, getting bogged down in questionable local state budget management, and then seeking to address the situation through a markedly status quo approach.

Finally, that Chinese investment is not necessarily exceptional is also evident when we consider that Chinese projects overseas are often built upon pre-existing developments initiated by other local or international corporations, facilitated by international financial institutions, and in some cases even implemented in partnership with Western companies. This can be seen, for instance, in how Chinese mining companies have repeatedly taken over controversial concessions from other Western companies. This is the case of the Toromocho copper mine in Peru, located in an area that had originally been mined at a small scale by companies of various origins, until a Canadian prospecting firm acquired concession rights in 2002 just to sell them to the Chinese Cinalco in 2007 (Lin, 2021). It is also the case of the Rio Blanco and Mirador mining projects in Ecuador, which were both initiated by Canadian companies in the late 1990s and then taken over by Chinese companies in the ensuing two decades (Initiative for Sustainable Investments China-Latin America, 2020a and 2020b). Similar dynamics can also be found in Asia, for instance in the controversial Letpadaung copper mine in Myanmar (Yu, 2021). In other contexts, Chinese companies have been able to come in and secure concessions thanks to external policy prescriptions of multilateral international institutions such as the International Monetary Fund and the World Bank, for instance in the case of Zambia, where debt relief assistance was made conditional on the privatisation of the copper industry, which had previously been nationalised (Lee, 2017; Li, 2010). Occasionally, Chinese companies and Western counterparts team up to push forward controversial projects. This is what is happening today in Papua New Guinea, where Canadian conglomerate Barrick Gold and China's Zijin Mining are jointly running the problematic Porgera gold mine, which has been marred by severe human rights abuse and environmental issues (Beattie, 2021). In East Africa, France's Total and the majority state-owned China National Offshore Oil Corporation Ltd (CNOOC) are planning to build the world's longest heated crude oil pipeline, running from Hoima in Uganda to the port of Tanga in Tanzania, despite local communities' and civil society's concerns regarding extensive displacement and impacts on the critical ecosystems of the Lake Victoria basin area. This pipeline links to CNOOC-developed gas fields, and the majority state-owned Industrial and Commercial Bank of China is advising CNOOC on project financing (Inclusive Development International, 2021).

There is an argument to be made for Chinese companies being exceptional in that, in some cases, they are more prone than others to take on uncertain, risky, and even unlikely projects that fit the geopolitical agenda of the Party-State. There is also evidence that Chinese companies and banks are less transparent and accountable than their peers from other countries (BHRRC, 2021). However, Chinese actors definitely do not operate in a void and are subject to similar logics and rules as their competitors (or their partners).

Eroding Labour Standards?

An idea that has gained currency in discourses on the exceptionality of Chinese investment and projects overseas is that Chinese investors are more likely to disregard existing local regulations in their quest to maximise profit and bring in their own workers, to the detriment of the local communities. The debates and the literature about labour rights on Chinese-invested projects overseas present a slightly more complicated picture.

In the Global South, local media often voice concerns about supposed 'invasions' of Chinese workers taking away job opportunities from local populations. For instance, in an article published in February 2019 with the headline 'How Come There Are So Many Chinese Workers Here?', the *Philippine Daily Inquirer* lamented the presence in the Philippines of between 200,000 and 400,000 Chinese workers, in competition with 2.3 million unemployed local people for jobs in the construction, mining, and entertainment sectors. A few months later, in June 2019, an article in the *South China Morning Post* wondered: 'Why Are Chinese Workers So Unpopular in Southeast Asia?' (Siu, 2019). Such discourses are often grounded in the decades-old ideas of Chinese labour as extremely cheap, when in fact there is evidence that Chinese companies in developing countries resort to workers imported from China when they face challenges to secure local manpower or have difficulties utilising local labour owing to language barriers or skill level (Chen, 2021). In Cambodia, for instance, we found that Chinese construction workers were paid between five and seven times as much as their local counterparts, even in situations in which they had to carry out basically the same tasks (Franceschini, 2020a).

In developed countries, there is plenty of anxiety about what takeovers by Chinese companies entail for local workers, feelings that have been well represented, for example in Netflix's 2019 documentary *American Factory* (Chan, 2019). Although this type of concern is generally articulated from the perspective of the local workforce, there is plenty of evidence that Chinese workers on Chinese projects overseas are not faring very well either (Halegua, 2022). For instance, Aaron Halegua (2020a and 2020b) has extensively documented the vicissitudes of thousands of Chinese workers working on the construction sites of a casino and luxury resort marketed as part of the BRI in Saipan, a US territory in the Pacific. Employed by different Chinese companies – both state-owned and private – these workers were promised well-paid jobs only to find themselves forced to work interminable shifts, for wages below the local legal minimum, and in precarious health and safety conditions, all the while being unable to return to China because the managers had taken away their passports and because of fears of arrest due to their irregular immigration status. In discussing the case, Halegua emphasises that, in the absence of trade unions, local media and international public opinion are of the utmost importance in addressing this kind of situation.

Zhang Shuchi (2018) has described the legal odyssey of a Chinese worker who was dispatched to a subsidiary of a Chinese-owned enterprise in Papua New Guinea. After suffering from serious health problems due to an attack by disgruntled local employees, this worker found himself unable to seek compensation from his employer because of the ambiguity of his employment relationship and the inadequacy of the Chinese regulations in this field. And the vagaries of China's labour dispatch system – which remains largely understudied, with only a few commendable exceptions such as the recent articles by legal scholars and practitioners Aaron Halegua and Xiaohui Ban (2020a and 2020b) – are also behind a couple of cases of Chinese and Vietnamese dispatch workers employed in awful conditions in important Chinese projects in Serbia that made headlines in 2021 (for a detailed discussion of these cases, see Matković, 2021). Finally, we ourselves have documented the situation in Chinese-owned construction sites in Sihanoukville, Cambodia, where both Chinese and Cambodian workers were often victims of agencies and subcontractors who resorted to predatory practices, until a ban on online gambling in 2019 led to the collapse of the local economy, leaving uncountable Chinese workers stranded owing to wage arrears and contractual traps (Franceschini, 2020a).

While all the abuses described above are undoubtedly true and should be denounced, there are at least two reasons to question the framing of these issues as a typical feature of 'Chinese capital'. First, existing research shows that Chinese investors are remarkably flexible in adapting to local circumstances.

Looking at Chinese investment in Europe, Yu Zheng and Chris Smith (2017, p. 31) have highlighted how in the European labour market Chinese companies have found 'more space to negotiate with existing institutional players (national states, trade unions, employment agents) to develop divergent employment practices', a process in which they have proven 'extremely pragmatic, adaptive, and willing to work with local institutions'. In a similar vein, in a survey conducted in 2017 on a sample of forty-two of approximately seventy Chinese-invested companies (including 'green field' investments) in the manufacturing, logistics, and service sectors in Germany, trade unionist Wolfgang Mueller (2018) concluded that after the entry of Chinese investors, the co-determination culture at the factory and company level, as well as the collective agreements, remained essentially unchanged or, in some cases, even improved. According to his findings, fears of widespread job losses did not materialise and while know-how is indeed being transferred to China, at the same time the research and development capacities have expanded in the Chinese-invested companies. If we compare these studies in European settings with the stories described above taking place in Saipan, Cambodia, and Papua New Guinea, there is an argument to be made that where local institutions and the rule of law are strong, Chinese investors tend to adapt; conversely, where institutions are weak and the law is scarcely implemented, they tend to take advantage of the situation to maximise profit to the detriment of the interests of the workers – a situation that is common among corporate actors around the world and in no way unique to Chinese capital.

Second, the very idea that there is such a thing as an organically coherent 'Chinese capital' is questionable. In the field of labour rights and industrial relations, Chris Smith and Yu Zheng (2016 and 2017) have challenged the very idea that there exist occupational practices that are typically 'Chinese', which can function as a model for Chinese companies overseas. Examining Chinese investment in the mining and construction sectors in Zambia, Ching Kwan Lee (2017) noticed some differences between Chinese state capital and international private capital. While both types of investors were not particularly benevolent towards workers, Chinese state companies in Zambia resorted to an employment model that Lee defines as 'stable exploitation', characterised by low salaries and relative stability, against the 'flexible exclusion' that could be found in private companies from other countries, where higher salaries were accompanied by higher precariousness. In explaining this difference on the basis of the different logics of accumulation behind the two types of capital – Chinese state investors tend to not only seek profit but also follow the political agenda of the Chinese Party-State and therefore are more sensitive to issues related to their public image, for instance – Lee shifted the attention from a racialised view of capital to a more nuanced understanding in which other criteria, such as ownership, determine its behaviour. Finally, drawing from her research in Ethiopia, Ding Fei (2021) has pointed out how the way that Chinese companies manage their employees is largely influenced by the type of company, its business model, local market conditions, and the support it receives from headquarters back in China.

Based on his research in the Caribbean, Ruben Gonzalez-Vicente (2020) has argued that to find differences between Chinese and other types of capital we should look at the 'predistribution stage' – that is, those enabling environments that allow capital to form and accumulate, which are not naturally pre-existing but rather established by government-to-government agreements involving Chinese diplomatic branches, policy banks, companies, and host country institutions. It is in this primary stage that there is some evidence of Chinese actors trying to change the rules of the game. In Serbia, for instance, the Hesteel Smederevo Steel Plant, acquired by the Chinese provincial state-owned enterprise Hesteel in 2016, successfully pressured the country's Ministry of Labour via the Chinese embassy to water down the legislation on sick leave rights (Rogelja, 2021). In Cambodia, we have documented how the Chinese trade union is engaging with government-aligned local unions, providing them with financial support and training opportunities, a situation which, when combined with the Cambodian government's crackdowns on independent unions, can potentially undermine the local labour movement (Franceschini, 2020b). However, cases in which China's clout is used to undermine existing labour standards remain an exception (at least for the time being) and an examination of the 'predistribution stage' most often shows that Chinese actors are subjected to the same pressures and rules as their competitors and those who came before them.

Towards a More Granular Understanding

In discussing the complexities underlying the idea of global (and Global) China, Ching Kwan Lee (2017, p. 161) warns against 'the facile resort to sweeping and grandiose generalization in terms of hegemony, empire, and neocolonialism', arguing for 'fine-grained, grounded empirical and comparative research'. To be able to do this, it is important that we taper the often unnuanced obsession with the BRI and start focussing instead on the actual behaviour of Chinese actors on the ground, making the effort to go beyond entrenched preconceptions to unearth hidden parallels and linkages, as well as the ways in which Chinese patterns of globalisation have evolved out of, and built on, pre-existing arrangements and formulations. While the scholarly debate – and, even more, media and policy discussions – remains dominated by perspectives that examine Chinese global engagements in geopolitical and macroeconomic terms, in recent years several young anthropologists and social scientists have produced excellent studies of how global China is experienced in various settings (in the labour field see, for instance, Driessen, 2019; Schmitz, 2020; Zhu, 2020; Chen, 2021; Hofman, 2021). There have also been efforts to build links between academia and civil society to create synergies to better document the social impact of Chinese projects overseas in a grounded, empirical perspective, including the pioneering, environment-focussed *China Dialogue* and our more recent experiment, *The People's Map of Global China*. While these studies and efforts will hardly produce a narrative as appealing as those put forward by the proponents of 'debt traps', 'silent invasions', or benevolent 'win-win' rhetoric and 'South–South co-operation', they might get us closer to understanding what global China really means for the people who experience it in their everyday lives and help us to better visualise the broader implications of Chinese globalisation going forward.

5 The Academe

We conclude this Element by turning our attention to the nexus between China and Western academia, which has become a heavily contested and controversial sphere. Since the late nineteenth century, foreign governments and religious societies have been sponsoring educational institutions in China with the ultimate objective to boost their political influence, spread Christianity, or for simple humanitarian reasons (Hayhoe, 1996). Peking University, which to this day remains China's foremost academic institution, was established in this fashion in 1898. In a similar vein, today's proponents of the 'maieutic approach' see increased Chinese participation in Western academia – mostly through the rapid growth of Chinese student numbers and research collaborations – and the involvement of Western academia in China as key tools in the broader strategy of 'educating' China in the norms and values of the liberal international system. However, in recent years universities, publishers, and researchers have found themselves embroiled in escalating scandals related to their collaborations with Chinese actors. This situation has resulted in Western academic engagements with China increasingly being depicted in negative terms – a discourse that is dominated by an essentialised vision of China as an external, corrupting force within the Western university.

In this section we examine some of the recent scandals and unpack their underlying dynamics. We start by focussing on the much-debated Confucius Institutes (CIs), then move on to examine other forms of partnership between

Western universities and Chinese actors (both universities and companies), and conclude the section with a reflection on how the commercial nature of much academic publishing today facilitates the demands for censorship from the Chinese Party-State.

Globalising the University with Chinese Characteristics (and Money)

Over the past decade, CIs have featured prominently in discussions about Chinese influence in international academia. Established in the early 2000s, the CIs are an educational institution aiming to promote the learning of Chinese language and culture worldwide and falling under the purview of China's Ministry of Education. Different from the German Goethe-Institut or the Spanish Instituto Cervantes – which are stand-alone institutions operating independently of universities – CIs integrate into universities and are formed as a partnership between a Chinese university and a foreign counterpart where the CI is housed, a mode of operation that Marshall Sahlins (2015) famously dubbed 'academic malware'. CIs have substantial flexibility and engage in different contractual arrangements based on local contexts, making it impossible to generalise about their practices globally (Repnikova, 2022). However, over the years CIs have been involved in a number of high-profile incidents related to free speech and academic freedom on campuses around the world. For instance, in 2009 North Carolina State University cancelled a talk by the Dalai Lama after alleged objections from the CI, and in 2013 a similar thing happened in Sydney (*Guardian*, 2013; *Washington Post*, 2014). Then in 2014 there was a major scandal at the European Association for Chinese Studies conference in Braga and Coimbra, Portugal – which was partly funded by the Hanban, the headquarters of all CIs – when then Director-General of the Hanban, Xu Lin, ordered the removal of the pages of the conference programme containing information about the Taiwanese Chiang Ching-kuo Foundation and Taiwan National Central Library, unbeknownst to the conference organisers (Greatrex, 2014).

While dramatic events like these are not uncommon, the more pernicious impact of the CIs on host universities is twofold. On one side, there is the risk of self-censorship around 'sensitive topics' by many of those involved with the CIs, which has served to subtly (or not so subtly) co-opt non-Chinese institutions into the PRC's wider project of 'telling the Chinese story well' (Barmé, 2012; Sahlins, 2015). On the other, given the scarcity of resources for activities on China-related issues in smaller universities, CIs often end up monopolising the discourse about China. In the absence of other sources of funding, universities often have to either accept the money offered by a CI or give up on the idea of having any instruction or activities related to China at all, to the detriment of both academic staff and students. As CIs tend to offer a positive (and, curiously, often orientalist) image of China – which is perfectly understandable considering the mission of these institutions, but no less problematic – this leads to obvious dilemmas. In an example of this type of dynamic, the Chinese co-director of a CI in a European university once openly offered one of us a substantial amount of funding to work on literary translations from Chinese, as long as he gave up conducting research on other, more politically sensitive issues – an offer that was obviously declined but which others might not have the luxury to refuse.

Considering these problems, it is unsurprising that many universities in Europe and North America are opting to shut down their CIs or not renew agreements, particularly in countries where relations with China are tense. It is equally unsurprising that CIs remain widespread, particularly in smaller and less well-funded institutions, and that they remain in high demand across the Global South (Repnikova, 2022). This is because for many institutions, having a CI is first and foremost a way to secure much-needed funding for Chinese language instruction and Chinese language resources. The CIs come with substantial start-up capital, as well as Chinese teachers and classroom materials (Repnikova, 2022). In some cases, the CIs also represent an opportunity to subcontract out the work of already existing China Studies departments in a bid to save money – a situation that occurred at Newcastle University in Australia and was met with pushback from both faculty and students (Sahlins, 2014). As a result of the structural shortcomings of the neoliberal academe in the West, CIs are able to incorporate themselves into universities and exert influence in more or less explicit ways depending on the place. As contracts are tailored to different institutions and the CIs often utilise non-disclosure agreements, the terms are generally not transparent (Hunter, 2019).

One of the more troubling aspects of this arrangement is the issue of new academic hires in China Studies programmes that collaborate with CIs. In recent years there have been numerous examples of universities putting out adverts for ongoing positions in China Studies, where the role is both university lecturer and the director or deputy director of the local CI. In this way, the CIs become directly involved in the vetting and hiring of academics who will not only direct the CI activities but also go on to shape the direction of China Studies at the universities going forward. While there are many excellent academics working on topics deemed acceptable by the CIs, in the current context, where academic positions are scarce and highly competitive, being able to influence hiring in China Studies has significant implications for the field. And there is certainly evidence to suggest that CIs do not shy away from imposing ideological demands on the hiring processes they are involved in. For instance, in 2012 McMaster University was forced to deal with a lawsuit from a CI teacher who was unable to keep her position when it was revealed that she was a follower of Falun Gong (Sahlins, 2014).

Other Controversial Collaborations

But CIs are not the only Chinese academic collaborations that potentially shape research and teaching on China in Western universities. Chinese government funding has been used to set up a range of different partnerships, centres, institutes, and so on, both within Western institutions and with Western institutions in China. For example, in 2018 Cambridge University's Jesus College established the UK-China Global Issues Dialogue Centre with a grant of 200,000 GBP from the Chinese government's National Development and Reform Commission. The College also received 155,000 GBP from Huawei and subsequently produced a white paper that portrayed the company in a flattering light (Fisher and Dunning, 2020). Jesus College also houses the offices of the Cambridge China Development Trust, an organisation that runs training programmes for CEOs of Chinese state-owned companies and government officials and which has received large donations from multinational corporations operating in China (Dunning et al., 2021). Finally, in 2018 the University established the Cambridge University-Nanjing Centre of Technology and Innovation with 10 million GBP of funding from the Chinese government. Located in Nanjing, this is Cambridge's first research centre established abroad and aims to foster research on smart cities and attract tech companies as partners. While there has not been any suggestion that this Centre has been involved in controversial research, in Section 3 we have seen how leading international academic institutions, including the Massachusetts Institute of Technology, have come under scrutiny for having research partnerships with artificial intelligence companies that have business ties with Chinese state security and other problematic actors involved in enhancing the Party-State's surveillance capabilities in Xinjiang, often under the very aegis of 'smart' or 'safe' cities projects (see also Byler, 2022a).

Similar questions linger about the overseas campuses of Western universities in China and, in rarer instances, prospective campuses of Chinese universities abroad. As an example of the latter situation, over the past year, plans to build a campus of Fudan University in Budapest, Hungary, while strongly supported by the Hungarian central government, have triggered a negative public reaction for a number of reasons, including an utter lack of transparency and many practical concerns regarding budgetary capacity (Strelcová, 2021). New York University Shanghai – a joint venture between NYU and East China Normal University established in 2012 and currently undergoing expansion – is a case in point of the former type of controversy. New York University has always insisted that academic freedom is a core principle of the Shanghai campus, with the community standards handbook saying: 'The University is a community where the means of seeking to establish truth are open discussion and free discourse. It thrives on debate and dissent, which must be protected as a matter of academic freedom within the University' (NYU Shanghai, 2019). However, recent interviews with NYU Shanghai faculty reveal that there is a general understanding that certain sensitive topics are not to be broached. In the words of an anonymous faculty member: 'Everyone is under a bit of a cloud of fear . . . there is a general idea that there are certain topics you don't discuss' (Levine, 2019). And the pressure to self-censor has been felt outside of Shanghai. Rebecca Karl – Professor of History at NYU in New York and one of the world's leading experts on modern Chinese intellectual history – has revealed that she is blacklisted from teaching at the Shanghai campus and that she had been told by fellow academics not to organise an event on protests in Hong Kong as it would be detrimental to colleagues in Shanghai (Levine, 2019). In response to these revelations, NYU Shanghai Associate Dean of Students Lauren Sinclair said: 'Here at NYU Shanghai, we speak with the intentionality not to be offensive' and 'NYU isn't trying to change places' (Barkenaes, 2020). This has led to questions about NYU's supposed commitment to the core academic principles of 'open discussion' and 'free discourse', and its mission 'to produce original, rigorous, and important insights . . . [that] promise to have a significant influence on the thinking of others'.

So how do we understand cases of Western academic institutions more or less covertly jettisoning commitments to academic freedom – and their implied mission to change the world for the better – in order to safeguard collaborations with, and funding from, Chinese political actors? Do these examples represent the unprecedented corrupting power of the CCP, with naive Western institutions entering into these partnerships in a good faith attempt to spread their liberal, democratic values into China only to find themselves compromised by the encounter? As Margaret Lewis (2021) has discussed in considerable detail, this would seem to be the essentialist perspective underpinning the US Department of Justice's 'China Initiative', which aims to identify scientific espionage in US universities. Unfortunately, in attempting to root out these 'corrupting forces' from China, innocent victims are caught up in the dragnet, as is the case with Chen Gang from the Massachusetts Institute of Technology and Hu Anming from the University of Tennessee – both of whom were prosecuted under the China Initiative for supposedly having ties to China. In both cases, the charges were dropped and the academics returned to their jobs, but not before suffering substantially both personally and professionally (Barry, 2022; Wright, 2022). These cases recall the dark days of the 1950s when an essentialised vision of a threatening China also loomed large and academics were similarly targeted for years of persecution (Lattimore, 1950).

The excesses of the China Initiative and much of the debate surrounding the malign influence of Chinese funding have not only been devastating for the innocent researchers targeted but ultimately have also obscured more fundamental issues plaguing the neoliberal university of today and undermined the cause of those who have been arguing for more efficient strategies to prevent problematic academic partnerships that might lead to IP theft or to the development of new technologies that might be used for repressive purposes (for a discussion, see, for instance, Darrowby, 2019). In fact, if we de-emphasise the 'Chineseness' of examples of 'Chinese influence' and instead shift our focus to the model of the neoliberal, managerial university – perpetually facing reduced budgets and focussed on vacuuming up as much external funding and tuition fees as possible – which currently dominates the Western academic landscape, we can then find innumerable examples that parallel the ones outlined above in their deleterious impacts on academic dynamics, but without Chinese actors involved.

For instance, we find private companies like Study Group that partner with universities to provide special courses 'to prepare' students for their undergraduate or master's studies (Study Group, n.d.). If students pass these expensive courses, then they can be admitted while bypassing certain parts of the normal admissions procedure. Like the CIs, companies like Study Group are external entities that enter and operate within the university structure without obvious oversight, taking advantage of budget gaps to achieve their aspirations. Also, both CIs and these companies hire their own staff, who are often not afforded the same protections as formal university employees, capitalising on and reinforcing the trend of creeping casualisation in academia.

We also find plenty of worrying examples of partnerships between academia and the military-industrial complex in the West, with Western universities receiving huge amounts of money from questionable stakeholders to pursue research with potential military and other ethically dubious applications (McCoy, 2014). Finally, there is no lack of instances of non-Chinese private actors aspiring to enter Western universities to promote their own ideological agendas and wield control over academic hiring. For instance, Charles Koch and his now-deceased brother David – owners of Koch Industries – have actively invested in financing research centres and other activities within universities aimed at pushing conservative policy agendas in the United States, prompting the 'UnKoch My Campus' campaign (UnKoch My Campus, n.d.). In 2021 Professor Beverly Gage resigned from the leadership of the prestigious Grand Strategy course at Yale University because of attempts by the programme's billionaire donors to influence curriculum and teaching – threatening funding withdrawal if they did not get their way (Schuessler, 2021).

Perhaps the most notorious case in point is that of the Ramsay Centre for Western Civilisation, which was set up in 2017 as part of the bequest of Australian businessman Paul Ramsay with the ambition to celebrate Western civilisation. The Ramsay Centre's overtures to a number of Australian universities caused much controversy and the offer was ultimately rejected by the Australian National University because of worries about academic integrity, as well as control over staffing and the curriculum (McGowan, 2018). However, this did not deter the University of Wollongong from accepting Ramsay funding to start a BA in Western Civilisation after confidential negotiations (University of Wollongong, 2019).

Read within this context, the CIs and other forms of 'Chinese influence' in Western academic institutions represent a symptom of the broader decay of neoliberal academia, which is the more fundamental problem that should be addressed. In arguing this, our point is not to downplay the fact that Chinese political actors are challenging some of the stated core values of Western academic institutions. Rather, it is to emphasise that, in explaining their existence and activities, we should look at how the Chinese examples parallel the ways in which a variety of external interests co-opt the neoliberal university – providing relatively minimal resources in exchange for access and the ability to drive research infrastructures built up over decades, often primarily with public money, in order to forward their agendas. And frequently these agendas are explicitly in contradiction to the values that these institutions still claim to uphold.

The Pitfalls of Commercial Academic Publishing

The commercialisation of academic publishing offers another example of how engagements with Chinese actors illuminate the general decay of neoliberal academia. In August 2017, it was revealed that Cambridge University Press (CUP) had capitulated to the Chinese censors, blocking access to 315 articles in *The China Quarterly*, one of the leading academic journals in China Studies (Phillips, 2017). At the time, this act of censorship was met with widespread protest and threats of a boycott, and, to its credit, CUP eventually reversed its decision (Kennedy and Phillips, 2017). It was soon discovered that CUP was not alone, as anonymous interviews with commercial publishers revealed widespread practices of self-censorship in China (*SCMP*, 2017). A few months later, in October 2017, Springer Nature – the world's largest academic publisher – admitted to 'limiting' at least 1,000 articles on their Chinese website at the request of the Chinese government. At that time, the publisher declared: 'We do not believe that it is in the interests of our authors, customers, or the wider scientific and academic community, or to the advancement of research for us to be banned from distributing our content in China' (Reuters, 2017). The following year, several scholars publicly complained that Springer Nature was removing 'politically sensitive' content published in the Transcultural Research book series from their Chinese website at the request of the Chinese authorities (MCLC, 2018). When confronted by the editors of the series, the publisher countered that they were merely following local laws and pointed to the fact that Chinese sales had increased in the wake of the act of self-censorship.

These incidents are widely interpreted as a dramatic demonstration of both China's increasing assertiveness and confidence and the lengths that academic publishers are willing to go to in order to maintain access to the Chinese market. However, while most commentators focus their indignation on the censoring practices of the Chinese authorities, it is our contention that such dynamics should be understood in the wider context of the academy's acquiescence to commercial modes of publishing that have turned the dissemination of scientific results into a highly profitable and exploitative business. Springer Nature has been at the forefront of the commercial revolution that in the post–World War II period saw academic publishing transformed from a varied landscape of small-scale journals and books published by a variety of institutions or professional societies into a vast market raking in higher profits than the leading tech companies of today. This profit is achieved through a 'triple-pay system' where the public: a) funds the research; b) funds the salaries of the authors, editors, and peer-reviewers; and c) purchases the published output through university library subscriptions (Buranyi, 2017). To make matters worse, the research is then locked behind outrageously expensive paywalls, making it inaccessible to the public that financed it in the first place (Monbiot, 2018). This system blocks access to academic research much more efficiently than any government censorship regime could dream of (Loubere and Franceschini, 2017). And, in fact, some corporate publishers are currently developing new forms of spyware to install on the proxy servers run by academic libraries in order to surveil users, ensuring that paywalls remain unbreached and profits secure (Mehta, 2020).

While the current situation is obviously absurd, particularly considering that the Internet allows for the easy and cheap dissemination of scientific findings, it is nevertheless a status quo that has proven very difficult to effectively contest. While there are open access movements, they often seek to operate through the existing publishing system, rather than outside it, for instance by paying publishers for the right to put articles online without any restriction. The profit-oriented publishing industry has been highly effective in limiting the space available to challenge its domination. Commercial entities control the journals, the citation indexes, and the official 'impact factors' that are used to rank journals. The ability to publish in the 'top journals' – as defined by this system – is crucial in order to find an academic job, achieve tenure, get promoted, and successfully apply for funding (Heckman and Moktan, 2018). Additionally, the number of articles published in top journals plays an important role in the university ranking systems (which are also commercially owned). This has made it extremely difficult for academics to extricate themselves from exploitative relationships with commercial academic publishers.

In this context, where academic subjugation to profit-oriented publishers is the normal state of affairs, commercial publishers opting to adhere to the demands of Chinese government censors or even pre-emptively self-censoring in order to ensure continued access to the Chinese market is unsurprising. After all, in a market system that prizes profits above all else, this decision makes perfect sense. Calls to boycott publishers in order to threaten their bottom line might work if their commercial interests are actually threatened by the boycott, but it only does so by feeding into the same profit-seeking mechanisms that prompted the bad behaviour in the first place. Equally, simply pointing the finger at the Chinese government for its successful attempts at censoring international academic publications risks obscuring the root cause that make such events possible – that is, a fundamental crisis in the mechanisms of academic publishing.

Beyond Dark Academia

Much has been written in recent years about the degeneration of universities into 'zombie' institutions working according to neoliberal logics and run by a 'dark academia' composed of bureaucrats only interested in reaching numerical targets and making a profit (Murphy, 2017; Fleming, 2021). This has had several implications. According to David Graeber (2015: 141), the commercialisation and bureaucratisation of academia have led to a shift from creative 'poetic technologies' that transform the status quo to 'bureaucratic technologies' which simply buttress it. As universities are bloated with 'bullshit jobs' and run by a managerial class that pits researchers against each other through countless rankings and evaluations, the very idea of academia as a place for pursuing groundbreaking ideas dies (Graeber, 2015, p. 135; 2018). With conformity and predictability now extolled as cardinal virtues, the purpose of the university is increasingly simply to confirm the obvious, develop technologies and knowledge of immediate relevance for the market, and exact astronomically high fees from students under the pretence of providing them with vocational training (hence the general attack on the humanities).

As Peter Fleming (2021, p. 5) has argued, we are now at a stage when corporatisation 'has been so exhaustive (on a financial, organisational, individual and subjective level) that reversing it in the current context feels nearly impossible. Rather than fighting back, most academics have merely found ways to dwell in the ruins'. In such a context, it is easy to see how key principles of academic life, such as 'academic freedom', have come to be substantially subverted (Franceschini, 2021). It is our conviction that the activities and influence of Chinese actors should be interpreted in this context – as yet another serious symptom of the terminal disease of the neoliberal university.

A Final Note

Over the past few years, we have had opportunities to present parts of this Element and some of the arguments that we advance in it to different audiences. On those occasions, we have often found ourselves stuck between a rock and a hard place, confronted by those holding 'essentialist' perspectives for allegedly downplaying the crimes of the Party-State by shifting focus to the dynamics of 'global capitalism', and also criticised by proponents of 'whataboutist' arguments for being blind to both the rapid progress in China and the shortcomings (and imperialist history) of the West. In other words, the argument that we put forward in this Element – that is, the crucial importance of contextualising the emergence of China as a key actor in longer-term histories of global capitalism and international engagement – does not fit neatly into the dominant frames of reference that exist for understanding either China's contentious domestic policies or its increasingly global presence.

As such, it is our conviction that a project of reconceptualising China in the world, or taking Global China as method, is an endeavour of crucial importance if we hope to come to grips with what Chinese globalisation in the twenty-first century means for our collective future. Global China as method thus entails a reimagining of China from a more contextualised global, historical, and relational perspective. It means acknowledging that China is not a discrete entity that can be analysed in isolation – an externality that exists outside of or beyond the 'real' world. Instead, taking Global China as method prompts us to focus our analytical lens not just on the particularity of 'Chinese phenomena' but rather on the processes underpinning Chinese globalisation – on the linkages and parallels, continuities and evolutions, as well as the ruptures, resulting from the intensification of Chinese entanglements in the global system.

As the discussions surrounding China become increasingly polarised between the 'essentialist' and 'whataboutist' frames (and with the 'maieutic' approach now seemingly in terminal decline but still deployed to justify the continuation of problematic partnerships under the pretence that the engagement is aimed at 'improving' China), with this Element we aim to provide a blueprint for a possible alternative approach to understanding China, which demonstrates that it is possible to remain highly critical of the policies adopted by the Chinese authorities in recent years – for example, the detention of hundreds of thousands of Uyghurs and other minorities, the crackdown on the labour movement, the ramping-up of surveillance, and the choice to censor critical content – while at the same time not losing sight of how these developments are embedded within, and reflective of, broader global trends. It is our belief that looking for these parallels, linkages, continuities, and evolutions is the necessary precondition for meaningful political action aimed at addressing the fundamental flaws of the system we all find ourselves living in.

References

Introduction

Dirlik, A. (2017). *Complicities: The People's Republic of China in Global Capitalism*. Chicago, IL: Prickly Paradigm Press.

Emirbayer, M. (1997). Manifesto for a Relational Sociology. *American Journal of Sociology*, 103(2), pp. 281–317.

Lee, C. K. (2017). *The Specter of Global China: Politics, Labor, and Foreign Investment in Africa*. Chicago, IL: University of Chicago Press.

Lee, G. B. (2018). *China Imagined: From European Fantasy to Spectacular Power*. London: Hurst Publishers.

Mizoguchi, Y. (translated by V. Murthy). ([1989]2016). China as Method. *Inter-Asia Cultural Studies*, 17(4), pp. 513–18.

Nyíri, P. and Breidenbach, J., eds. (2013). *China Inside Out: Chinese Nationalism and Transnationalism*. Budapest: Central European University Press.

Teng, B. 滕彪. (2020). 中美比较如何成为一种病毒 [How Comparisons between the United States and China Became a Virus]. 纽约时报中文网 [*The New York Times Chinese Website*], 28 May. https://cn.nytimes.com/opinion/20200528/coronavirus-china-us-pandemic.

Thomas, P. (2020). Trump Backed Xi over Concentration Camps for Uighur Muslims, Ex-aide Bolton Claims. *Independent*, 17 June. www.independent.co.uk/news/world/americas/us-politics/trump-uighur-muslims-concentration-camps-xi-china-john-bolton-book-a9571921.html.

Weber, I. M. (2020). Could the US and Chinese Economies Really 'Decouple'? *The Guardian*, 11 September. www.theguardian.com/commentisfree/2020/sep/11/us-china-global-economy-donald-trump.

Weber, I. M. (2021). *How China Escaped Shock Therapy: The Market Reform Debate*. Abingdon, UK: Routledge.

1 Chinese Labour in a Global Perspective

AmCham Shanghai. (2006). Labor Contract Law Comments to NPC (April 2006). The document is no longer available online.

Andreas, J. (2019). *Disenfranchised: The Rise and Fall of Industrial Citizenship in China*. New York: Oxford University Press.

Chan, A. (2001). *China's Workers under Assault: The Exploitation of Labor in a Globalizing Economy*. New York: M. E. Sharpe.

Chan, A. (2003). A 'Race to the Bottom': Globalization and China's Labour Standards. *China Perspectives*, 46, pp. 1–13.

Chan, A. (2022). Voices from the Zhili Fire: The Tragedy of a Toy Factory and the Conditions It Exposed. In I. Franceschini and C. Sorace, eds., *Proletarian China: A Century of Chinese Labour*. London: Verso Books, pp. 506–13.

Chan, A. and Siu, K. (2012). Chinese Migrant Workers: Factors Constraining the Emergence of Class Consciousness. In B. Carrillo and D. S. G. Goodman, eds., *Workers and Peasants in the Transformation of Urban China*. Cheltenham, UK: Edward Elgar, pp. 79–101.

Chan, C. K. (2013). Community-Based Organizations for Migrant Workers' Rights: The Emergence of Labour NGOs in China. *Community Development Journal*, 48(1), pp. 6–22.

Chan, C. K. (2014). Constrained Labour Agency and the Changing Regulatory Regime in China. *Development and Change*, 45(4), pp. 685–709.

Chan, J. (2022). The Foxconn Suicide Express. In I. Franceschini and C. Sorace, eds., *Proletarian China: A Century of Chinese Labour*. London: Verso Books, pp. 626–35.

Chen, B., Liu, T., and Wang, Y. (2020). Volatile Fragility: New Employment Forms and Disrupted Employment Protection in the New Economy. *International Journal of Environmental Research and Public Health*, 17(5): 1531.

Chen, E. (2021). These Chinese Millennials Are 'Chilling' and Beijing Isn't Happy. *The New York Times*, 3 July. www.nytimes.com/2021/07/03/world/asia/china-slackers-tangping.html.

Chen, F. (2016). China's Road to the Construction of Labor Rights. *Journal of Sociology*, 52(1), pp. 24–38.

Chen, F. and Yang, X. (2017). Movement-Oriented Labour NGOs in South China: Exit with Voice and Displaced Unionism. *China Information*, 31(1), pp. 155–75.

China Labour Bulletin. (2014). No More Delay: The Urgent Task of Implementing Collective Bargaining in Guangdong. *China Labour Bulletin*, 20 May. https://clb.org.hk/content/no-more-delay-urgent-task-implementing-collective-bargaining-guangdong.

Day, M. (2021). China's Downwardly Mobile Millennials Are Throwing In the Towel. *Jacobin*, 25 June. https://jacobinmag.com/2021/06/chinese-students-white-collar-workers-millennials-lying-flat-tang-ping.

Elfstrom, M. (2021). *Workers and Change in China: Resistance, Repression, Responsiveness*. New York: Cambridge University Press.

Feng, E. (2021). He Tried to Organize Workers in China's Gig Economy: Now He Faces 5 Years in Jail. *NPR*, 13 April. www.npr.org/2021/04/13/984994360/

he-tried-to-organize-workers-in-chinas-gig-economy-now-he-faces-5-years-in-jail.

Franceschini, I. (2009). The New Labour Contract Law of the People's Republic of China: A Real Step Forward for Chinese Trade Unions? Centro Alti Studi sulla Cina Contemporanea working paper. No longer available online but on record with the authors.

Franceschini, I. (2016). *Lavoro e diritti in Cina: Politiche sul lavoro e attivismo operaio nella fabbrica del mondo* [*Labour and Rights in China: Labour Policies and Worker Activism in the World Factory*]. Bologna: Il Mulino.

Franceschini, I. and Lin, K. (2019). Labour NGOs in China: From Legal Mobilisation to Collective Struggle (and Back?). *China Perspectives*, 2019 (1), pp. 75–84.

Franceschini, I. and Nesossi, E. (2016). The Foreign NGOs Management Law: A Compendium. *Made in China Journal*, 1(2), pp. 34–41.

Franceschini, I. and Nesossi, E. (2018). State Repression of Chinese Labor NGOs: A Chilling Effect? *The China Journal*, 80, pp. 111–29.

Friedman, E. (2014). *Insurgency Trap: Labor Politics in Postsocialist China*. Ithaca, NY: Cornell University Press.

Froissart, C. (2018). Negotiating Authoritarianism and Its Limits: Worker-Led Collective Bargaining in Guangdong Province. *China Information*, 32(1), pp. 23–45.

Gallagher, M. E. (2005). *Contagious Capitalism: Globalization and the Politics of Labour in China*. Princeton, NJ: Princeton University Press.

Gallagher, M. E. (2007). Hope for Protection and Hopeless Choices: Labor Legal Aid in the PRC. In E. Perry and M. Goldman, eds., *Grassroots Political Reform in Contemporary China*. Cambridge, MA: Harvard University Press, pp. 196–227.

Gallagher, M. E. (2017). *Authoritarian Legality: Law, Workers, and the State*. Cambridge: Cambridge University Press.

Gallagher, M. E. (2022). The Labour Contract Law and Its Discontents. In I. Franceschini and C. Sorace, eds., *Proletarian China: A Century of Chinese Labour*. London: Verso Books, pp. 587–98.

Gallagher, M. E. and Dong, B. (2011). Legislating Harmony: Labor Law Reform in Contemporary China. In S. Kuruvilla, C. K. Lee, and M. E. Gallagher, eds., *From Iron Rice Bowl to Informalization: Markets, Workers and the State in a Changing China*. Ithaca, NY: Cornell University Press, pp. 36–60.

Gallagher, M. E., Giles, J., Park, A., and Wang, M. (2015). China's 2008 Labor Contract Law: Implementation and Implications for China's Workers. *Human Relations*, 68(2), pp. 197–235.

Geng, Y. and Zhou, C. (2012). 劳动合同法修正案征得55万意见 [Draft Labour Contract Law Amendment Receives Over 550,000 Comments]. 21世纪经济报道 [*21ˢᵗ Century Business Herald*], 8 August, p. 6.

Guan, H. (2007). 构建和谐劳动关系与劳动法制建设 [The Establishment of Harmonious Labour Relations and the Edification of the Labour Law System]. 法学杂志 [*Law Review*], 3, pp. 29–32.

Harper, P. (1969). The Party and the Unions in Communist China. *The China Quarterly*, 37, pp. 84–119.

Howell, J. (2022). From Green Shoots to Crushed Petals: Labour NGOs in China. In I. Franceschini and C. Sorace, eds., *Proletarian China: A Century of Chinese Labour*. London: Verso Books, pp. 526–34.

Hui, E. S. (2017). *Hegemonic Transformation: The State, Laws, and Labour Relations in Post-Socialist China*. New York: Palgrave Macmillan.

Hui, E. S. and Chan, C. K. (2016). The Influence of Overseas Business Associations on Law-Making in China: A Case Study. *The China Quarterly*, 225, pp. 145–68.

Jiang, Y. (2012). 劳动合同法修改二审推延 [The Second Phase of the Labour Contract Law Amendment Is Delayed]. 经济观察网 [*The Economic Observer*], 27 October. http://finance.sina.com.cn/roll/20121027/065013498848.shtml.

Lee, C. K. (2007). *Against the Law: Labor Protests in China's Rustbelt and Sunbelt*. Berkeley, CA: University of California Press.

Lee, C. K. and Shen, Y. (2011). The Anti-Solidarity Machine? Labor Nongovernmental Organizations in China. In S. Kuruvilla, C. K. Lee, and M. E. Gallagher, eds., *From Iron Rice Bowl to Informalization: Markets, Workers and the State in a Changing China*. Ithaca, NY: Cornell University Press, pp. 173–87.

Lin, K. (2022). The Blocked Path: Political Labour Organising in the Aftermath of the Tiananmen Crackdown. In I. Franceschini and C. Sorace, eds., *Proletarian China: A Century of Chinese Labour*. London: Verso Books, pp. 535–44.

Shi, J. (2006). New Labour Law Would Bring Conflicts, European Firms Fear. *South China Morining Post*, 22 April.

Siu, K. (2020). *Chinese Migrant Workers and Employer Domination: Comparisons with Hong Kong and Vietnam*. Singapore: Palgrave Macmillan.

Snape, H. (2021). Cultivate Aridity and Deprive Them of Air: Altering the Approach to Non-State-Approved Social Organisations. *Made in China Journal*, 6(1), pp. 54–9.

Van Der Sprenkel, S. (1983). Labor Legislation of the Chinese Soviet Republic. In W. E. Butler, ed., *The Legal System of the Chinese Soviet Republic*. New York: Transnational Publishers, pp. 107–13.

Xu, Y. (2013). Labor Non-Governmental Organizations in China: Mobilizing Rural Migrant Workers. *Journal of Industrial Relations*, 55(2), pp. 243–59.

Zhang, Y. (2022). Workers on Tiananmen Square. In I. Franceschini and C. Sorace, eds., *Proletarian China: A Century of Chinese Labour*. London: Verso Books, pp. 496–505.

Zhou, I. (2020). *Digital Labour Platforms and Labour Protection in China*. ILO Working Paper 11. Geneva: International Labour Organization. www.ilo.org/wcmsp5/groups/public/–asia/–ro-bangkok/–ilo-beijing/documents/publication/wcms_757923.pdf.

2 Digital Dystopias

Arns, N. (2018). Prof. Muhammad Yunus on The New Economics of Zero Poverty, Zero Unemployment & Zero Net Carbon Emissions. *Impact Boom*, 14 December. www.impactboom.org/blog/2018/12/24/muhammad-yunus-on-the-new-economics-of-zero-poverty-zero-unemployment-zero-net-carbon-emissions.

Backer, L. C. (2018). And an Algorithm to Bind Them All? Social Credit, Data Driven Governance, and the Emergence of an Operating System for Global Normative Orders. SSRN Scholarly Paper ID 3182889. Rochester, NY: Social Science Research Network. https://doi.org/10.2139/ssrn.3182889.

Bislev, A. (2017). Contextualizing China's Online Credit Rating System. *China Policy Institute: Analysis*, 4 December. https://cpianalysis.org/2017/12/04/contextualizing-chinas-online-credit-rating-system.

Bratton, B. (2021). *The Revenge of the Real: Politics for a Post-Pandemic World*. London: Verso Books.

Carney, M. (2018). 'Leave No Dark Corner'. *ABC News*, 18 September. www.abc.net.au/news/2018-09-18/china-social-credit-a-model-citizen-in-a-digital-dictatorship/10200278.

Chelwa, G. and Muller, S. (2019). The Poverty of Poor Economics. *Africa Is a Country*, 17 October. https://africasacountry.com/2019/10/the-poverty-of-poor-economics.

Clover, C. (2016). China: When Big Data Meets Big Brother. *Financial Times*, 19 January. www.ft.com/content/b5b13a5e-b847-11e5-b151-8e15c9a029fb.

Daum, J. (2017). China Through a Glass, Darkly. *China Law Translate*, 24 December. www.chinalawtranslate.com/seeing-chinese-social-credit-through-a-glass-darkly/?lang=en.

Daum, J. (2019). Untrustworthy: Social Credit Isn't What You Think It Is. *Verfassungsblog*, 27 June. https://verfassungsblog.de/untrustworthy-social-credit-isnt-what-you-think-it-is.

Economist. (2016a). China Invents the Digital Totalitarian State. *The Economist*, 17 December. www.economist.com/news/briefing/21711902-worrying-implications-its-social-credit-project-china-invents-digital-totalitarian.

Economist. (2016b). China's Digital Dictatorship. *The Economist*, 17 December. www.economist.com/news/leaders/21711904-worrying-experiments-new-form-social-control-chinas-digital-dictatorship.

Economist. (2016c). Test of Character. *The Economist*, 29 September. www.economist.com/news/finance-and-economics/21707978-how-personality-testing-could-help-financial-inclusion-tests-character.

General Office of the State Council. (2016). 国务院办公厅关于加强个人诚信体系建设的指导意见 [The General Office of the State Council's Guiding Opinion on the Strengthening of the Establishment of the Personal Creditworthiness System]. China's State Council website, 30 December. www.gov.cn/zhengce/content/2016-12/30/content_5154830.htm.

Heilmann, S. (2008). From Local Experiments to National Policy: The Origins of China's Distinctive Policy Process. *The China Journal*, 59, pp. 1–30.

Loubere, N. (2017). China's Internet Finance Boom and Tyrannies of Inclusion. *China Perspectives*, 2017/4, pp. 9–18.

Loubere, N. (2019). *Development on Loan: Microcredit and Marginalisation in Rural China*. Amsterdam: Amsterdam University Press.

Loubere, N. (2021). Debt as Surveillance. *Progressive International*. 13 April, https://progressive.international/blueprint/05b4dc99-aa22-42ac-9839-56af1863c7ed-debt-as-surveillance/en.

Loubere, N. and Brehm, S. (2018). The Global Age of Algorithm: Social Credit and the Financialisation of Governance in China. *Made in China Journal*, 3 (1), pp. 38–42.

Matsakis, L. (2019). How the West Got China's Social Credit System Wrong. *Wired*, 29 July. www.wired.com/story/china-social-credit-score-system.

Palin, M. (2018). China's 'Social Credit' System Is a Real-Life 'Black Mirror' Nightmare. *New York Post*, 19 September. https://nypost.com/2018/09/19/chinas-social-credit-system-is-a-real-life-black-mirror-nightmare.

Privacy International. (2018). Fintech's Dirty Little Secret? Lenddo, Facebook and the Challenge of Identity. *Privacy International*, 23 October. http://privacyinternational.org/long-read/2323/fintechs-dirty-little-secret-lenddo-facebook-and-challenge-identity.

Reisinger, D. (2015). Why Facebook Profiles Are Replacing Credit Scores. *Fortune*, 2 December. https://fortune.com/2015/12/01/tech-loans-credit-affirm-zest.

State Council. (2014). 国务院关于印发社会信用体系建设规划纲要 (2014 – 2020年) 的通知

[Planning Outline for the Construction of a Social Credit System (2014–2020]. China's State Council website, 27 June. www.gov.cn/zhengce/content/2014-06/27/content_8913.htm.

Villarreal, D. (2021). What Top Republicans Are Saying about Vaccine Passports. *Newsweek*, 30 March. www.newsweek.com/what-top-republicans-are-saying-about-vaccine-passports-1579984.

World Bank. (2015). *World Development Report 2015: Mind, Society, and Behavior*. Washington DC: The World Bank.

Zeng, M. J. (2018). China's Social Credit System Puts Its People Under Pressure to Be Model Citizens. *The Conversation*, 23 January. http://theconversation.com/chinas-social-credit-system-puts-its-people-under-pressure-to-be-model-citizens-89963.

Zhang, C. (2020). Governing (through) Trustworthiness: Technologies of Power and Subjectification in China's Social Credit System. *Critical Asian Studies*, 52(4), pp. 565–88.

3 Xinjiang

Amy, J. and Rowlands S. (2018). Legalised Non-Consensual Sterilisation: Eugenics Put into Practice before 1945, and the Aftermath. Part 1: USA, Japan, Canada and Mexico. *The European Journal of Contraceptive & Reproductive Health Care*, (23)2, pp. 121–9.

Benns, W. (2015). American Slavery, Reinvented. *The Atlantic*, 21 September. www.theatlantic.com/business/archive/2015/09/prison-labor-in-america/406177.

Better Cotton Initiative (BCI). 2020. BCI to Cease All Field-Level Activities in the Xinjiang Uyghur Autonomous Region of China. *Announcements*, 21 October. Geneva: Better Cotton Initiative. http://web.archive.org/web/20210107110309/https://bettercotton.org/bci-to-cease-all-field-level-activities-in-the-xinjiang-uyghur-autonomous-region-of-china.

Bloomberg. (2019). Frontier Services Group Ltd (500: Stock Exchange of Hong Kong Limited). *Bloomberg*. www.bloomberg.com/research/stocks/people/person.asp?personId=242634425&capId=2482088&previousCapId=242505502&previousTitle=China Xinjiang Beixin Construction %26 Engineering (Group) Co. Ltd.

Brophy, D. (2019). Good and Bad Muslims in Xinjiang. *Made in China Journal*, 4(2), pp. 44–53.

Byler, D. (2019a). How Companies Profit from Forced Labor in Xinjiang. *SupChina*, 4 September. https://supchina.com/2019/09/04/how-companies-profit-from-forced-labor-in-xinjiang.

Byler, D. (2019b). Preventative Policing as Community Detention in Northwest China. *Made in China Journal*, 4(3), pp. 88–94.

Byler, D. (2020). The Global Implications of 'Re-education' Technologies in Northwest China. *Center for Global Policy*, 8 June. https://cgpolicy.org/articles/the-global-implications-of-re-education-technologies-in-northwest-china.

Byler, D. (2022a). Surveillance, Data Police, and Digital Enclosure in Xinjiang's 'Safe Cities'. In D. Byler, I. Franceschini, and N. Loubere, eds., *Xinjiang Year Zero*. Canberra: ANU Press, pp. 176–96.

Byler, D. (2022b). *Terror Capitalism: Uyghur Dispossession and Masculinity in a Chinese City*. Durham, NC: Duke University Press.

Byler, D., Franceschini, I., and Loubere, N. (2022). *Xinjiang Year Zero*. Canberra: ANU Press.

Cheek, T. (2019). Thought Reform. In C. Sorace, I. Franceschini, and N. Loubere, eds., *Afterlives of Chinese Communism: Political Concepts from Mao to Xi*. Canberra: ANU Press and Verso Books, pp. 287–92.

Cliff, T. (2016). *Oil and Water: Being Han in Xinjiang*. Chicago, IL: University of Chicago Press.

Cole, M. and Scahill, J. (2016). Eric Prince in the Hot Seat. *The Intercept*, 24 March. https://theintercept.com/2016/03/24/blackwater-founder-erik-prince-under-federal-investigation.

Darrowby, J. (2019). Intellectual Property, Artificial Intelligence, and Ethical Dilemmas: China and the New Frontiers of Academic Integrity. *Made in China Journal*, 4(1), pp. 24–9.

Dirlik, A. (2017). *Complicities: The People's Republic of China in Global Capitalism*. Chicago, IL: Prickly Paradigm Press.

Fan, L. (2017). Blackwater Founder to Open Bases in Xinjiang. *The Global Times*, 21 March. www.globaltimes.cn/content/1038847.shtml.

Franceschini, I. and Byler, D. (2021). Primo Levi, Camp Power, and Terror Capitalism: A Conversation with Darren Byler. *Made in China Journal*, 6(2), pp. 272–81.

Frontier Services Group (FSG). (2017). Annual Report 2017. http://doc.irasia.com/listco/hk/frontier/annual/2017/ar2017.pdf.

Greitens, S. C., Lee, M., and Yazici, E. (2020). Counterterrorism and Preventive Repression: China's Changing Strategy in Xinjiang. *International Security*, 44(3), pp. 9–47.

Harney, A. (2019). Risky Partner: Top U.S. Universities Took Funds from Chinese Firms Tied to Xinjiang Security. *Reuters*, 13 June. www.reuters.com/article/us-china-xinjiang-mit-tech-insight-idUSKCN1TE04M.

Hu, K. and Dastin, J. (2020). Amazon Turns to Chinese Firm on U.S. Blacklist to Meet Thermal Camera Needs. *Reuters*, 29 April. www.reuters.com/article/us-health-coronavirus-amazon-com-cameras/exclusive-amazon-turns-to-chinese-firm-on-u-s-blacklist-to-meet-thermal-camera-needs-idUSKBN22B1AL.

Marcus, A. (2020). Study of China's Ethnic Minorities Retracted as Dozens of Papers Come Under Scrutiny for Ethical Violations. *Retraction Watch*, 6 August. https://retractionwatch.com/2020/08/06/study-of-chinas-ethnic-minorities-retracted-as-dozens-of-papers-come-under-scrutiny-for-ethical-violations.

McNeill, S., McGregor, J., McGriffiths, M., Walsh, M., and Hui, E. (2019). UTS, Curtin Unis Announce Reviews over Links to Surveillance Tech Used by Chinese Government. *ABC News Four Corners*, 16 July. www.abc.net.au/news/2019-07-16/australian-unis-to-review-links-to-chinese-surveillance-tech/11309598.

Monbiot, G. (2020). Boris Johnson Says We Shouldn't Edit Our Past. But Britain Has Been Lying about It for Decades. *The Guardian*, 16 June. www.theguardian.com/commentisfree/2020/jun/16/boris-johnson-lying-history-britain-empire.

Nemser, D. (2017). *Infrastructures of Race: Concentration and Biopolitics in Colonial Mexico*. Austin: University of Texas Press.

Nguyen, M. T. (2012). *The Gift of Freedom: War, Debt, and Other Refugee Passages*. Durham, NC: Duke University Press.

Ordonez, V. (2019). Erik Prince's Company Plans Business in China Province under Human Rights Scrutiny According to Financial Disclosure. *ABC News*, 10 October. https://abcnews.go.com/International/erik-princes-company-plans-business-china-province-human/story?id=66139535.

Patton, D. (2016). Xinjiang Cotton at Crossroads of China's New Silk Road. *Reuters*, 12 January. www.reuters.com/article/us-china-xinjiang-cotton-insight-idUSKCN0UQ00320160112.

Pitzer, A. (2018). *One Long Night: A Global History of Concentration Camps*. New York: Little, Brown and Company.

Roberts, S. (2020). *The War on the Uyghurs: China's Internal Campaign Against a Muslim Minority*. Princeton, NJ: Princeton University Press.

Robertson, M. (2020). Counterterrorism or Cultural Genocide? Theory and Normativity in Knowledge Production About China's 'Xinjiang Strategy'. *Made in China Journal*, 5(2), pp. 72–81.

Roche, G. (2019). Transnational Carceral Capitalism in Xinjiang and Beyond. *Made in China Journal*, 4(1), pp. 13–15.

Rollet, C. (2019). Influential US Scientist under Fire for Xinjiang Links. *Coda*, 12 September. www.codastory.com/authoritarian-tech/influential-us-scientist-under-fire-xinjiang-links.

Salimjan, G. (2022). Camp Land: Settler Ecotourism and Kazakh Removal in Contemporary Xinjiang. In D. Byler, I. Franceschini, and N. Loubere, eds., *Xinjiang Year Zero*. Canberra: ANU Press, pp. 140–56.

Shepherd, C. (2019). Erik Prince Company to Build Training Centre in China's Xinjiang. *Reuters*, 31 January. www.reuters.com/article/us-china-xinjiang/erik-prince-company-to-build-training-center-in-chinas-xinjiang-idUSKCN1PP169.

Sorace, C. (2020). Gratitude: The Ideology of Sovereignty in Crisis. *Made in China Journal*, 5(2), pp. 166–9.

Sorace, C. (2021). The Chinese Communist Party's Nervous System: Affective Governance from Mao to Xi. *The China Quarterly*, first view. https://doi.org/10.1017/S0305741021000680.

Thum, R. (2020). The Spatial Cleansing of Xinjiang: *Mazar* Desecration in Context. *Made in China Journal*, 4(2), pp. 48–61.

Todorov, T. (1986). Prefazione [Preface]. In P. Levi, *I sommersi e i salvati* [*The Drowned and the Saved*]. Turin: Einaudi, pp. v–xi.

Wee, S.-L. (2019). China Uses DNA to Track Its People, With the Help of American Expertise. *New York Times*, 21 February. www.nytimes.com/2019/02/21/business/china-xinjiang-uighur-dna-thermo-fisher.html

Wee, S.-L. (2021). Two Scientific Journals Retract Articles Involving Chinese DNA Research. *The New York Times*, 9 September. www.nytimes.com/2021/09/09/business/china-dna-retraction-uyghurs.html.

Xu, V. X., Cave, D., Leibold, J., Munro, K., and Ruser, N. (2020). Uyghurs for Sale: 'Re-education', Forced Labour and Surveillance beyond Xinjiang. Australian Strategic Policy Institute, 1 March. www.aspi.org.au/report/uyghurs-sale.

Yi, X. (2019). Blood Lineage. In C. Sorace, I. Franceschini, and N. Loubere, eds., *Afterlives of Chinese Communism: Political Concepts from Mao to Xi*. Canberra: ANU Press, pp. 17–22.

4 Belts and Roads

Beattie, E. (2021). China-Backed Mining Deepens Papua New Guinea's Golden Dilemma. *Asia Nikkei*, 24 August. https://asia.nikkei.com/Spotlight/Asia-Insight/China-backed-mining-deepens-Papua-New-Guinea-s-golden-dilemma.

Bräutigam, D. (2009). *The Dragon's Gift: The Real Story of China in Africa*. Oxford: Oxford University Press.

Business and Human Rights Resource Centre (BHRRC). (2021). 'Going Out' Responsibly: The Human Rights Impact of China's Global Investment.

BHRRC website. www.bhrrc.org/en/from-us/briefings/going-out-responsibly-the-human-rights-impact-of-chinas-global-investments.

Chan, A. (2019). *American Factory*: Clash of Cultures or Clash of Labour and Capital? *Made in China Journal*, 5(1), pp. 174–9.

Chen, K. W. (2021). Railroaded: The Financial Politics and the Labour Puzzle of Global China. *Made in China Journal*, 6(1), pp. 132–7.

Cheng, P. (2021). Shwe Kokko Special Economic Zone / Yatai New City. *The People's Map of Global China*, 31 March. https://thepeoplesmap.net/project/shwe-kokko-special-economic-zone-yatai-new-city.

Driessen, M. (2019). *Tales of Hope, Tastes of Bitterness: Chinese Road Builders in Ethiopia*. Hong Kong: Hong Kong University Press.

Fei, D. (2021). Chinese Companies Have Different Ways of Managing Africa Employees. *The Washington Post*, 9 April. www.washingtonpost.com/politics/2021/04/09/chinese-companies-have-different-ways-managing-african-employees.

Franceschini, I. (2020a). 'As Far Apart as Earth and Sky': A Survey of Chinese and Cambodian Construction Workers in Sihanoukville. *Critical Asian Studies*, 52(4), pp. 512–29.

Franceschini, I. (2020b). The Chinese Trade Union Goes Global: Evidence from Cambodia. *China Perspectives*, 4/2020, pp. 29–37.

Galway, M. (2021). Who Are Our Friends? Maoist Cultural Diplomacy and the Origins of the People's Republic of China's Global Turn. *Made in China Journal*, 6(2), pp. 110–25.

Galway, M. (2022). Building Uhuru: Chinese Workers and Labour Diplomacy on the Tam–Zam Railway. In I. Franceschini and C. Sorace, eds., *Proletarian China: A Century of Chinese Labour*. London: Verso Books, pp. 416–26.

Garlick, J. (2019). *The Impact of China's Belt and Road Initiative: From Asia to Europe*. Abingdon, UK: Routledge.

Gonzalez-Vicente, R. (2020). Varieties of Capital and Predistribution: The Foundations of Chinese Infrastructural Investment in the Caribbean. *Made in China Journal*, 5(1), pp. 164–9.

Halegua, A. (2020a). From Africa to Saipan: What Happens When Chinese Construction Firms 'Go Global'? *Made in China Journal*, 5(1), pp. 160–3.

Halegua, A. (2020b). Where is China's Belt and Road Leading International Labour Rights? An Examination of Worker Abuse by Chinese Construction Firms in Saipan. In M. A. Carrai and J. Wouters, eds., *The Belt and Road Initiative and Global Governance*. Cheltenham, UK: Edward Elgar Publishing, pp. 225–57.

Halegua, A. (2022). Chinese Workers on the Belt and Road. In I. Franceschini and C. Sorace, eds., *Proletarian China: A Century of Chinese Labour*. London: Verso Books, pp. 645–55.

Halegua, A. and Ban, X. (2020a). Labour Protections for Overseas Chinese Workers: Legal Framework and Judicial Practice. *The Chinese Journal of Comparative Law*, 8(2), pp. 304–30.

Halegua, A. and Ban, X. (2020b). Legal Remedies for China's Overseas Workers. *Made in China Journal*, 5(3), pp. 86–91.

Heilmann, S. (2008). From Local Experiments to National Policy: The Origins of China's Distinctive Policy Process. *The China Journal*, 59, pp. 1–30.

Hofman, I. (2021). In the Interstices of Patriarchal Order: Spaces of Female Agency in Chinese–Tajik Labour Encounters. *Made in China Journal*, 6(2), pp. 202–9.

Hong, E. and Sun, L. (2006). Dynamics of Internationalization and Outward Investment: Chinese Corporations' Strategies. *The China Quarterly*, 187, pp. 610–34.

Inclusive Development International. (2020). Time to Raise the Bar: Reflecting on Four Years of AIIB Projects. Inclusive Development International website. www.inclusivedevelopment.net/wp-content/uploads/2020/05/aiib-briefer-time-to-raise-the-bar-web-version.pdf.

Inclusive Development International. (2021). East African Crude Oil Pipeline. *The People's Map of Global China*, 30 March. https://thepeoplesmap.net/project/east-africa-crude-oil-pipeline.

Initiative for Sustainable Investments China-Latin America. (2020a). Mirador Mining Project. *The People's Map of Global China*, 3 November. https://thepeoplesmap.net/project/mirador-mining-project.

Initiative for Sustainable Investments China-Latin America. (2020b). Rio Blanco Mining Project. *The People's Map of Global China*, 3 November. https://thepeoplesmap.net/project/rio-blanco-mining-project.

Jones, L. and Zeng, J. (2019). Understanding China's 'Belt and Road Initiative': Beyond Grand Strategy to a 'State Transformation' Analysis. *Third World Quarterly*, 40(8), pp. 1415–39.

Lee, C. K. (2017). *The Specter of Global China: Politics, Labor, and Foreign Investment in Africa*. Chicago, IL: The University of Chicago Press.

Li, P. (2010). The Myth and Reality of Chinese Investors: A Case Study of Chinese Investment in Zambia's Copper Industry. China in Africa Project occasional paper, no. 62. https://media.africaportal.org/documents/SAIIA_Occasional_Paper_62.pdf.

Lin, Z. (2021). Toromocho Copper Mine Project. *The People's Map of Global China*, 31 March. https://thepeoplesmap.net/project/toromocho-copper-mine-project.

Loubere, N., Lu, J., Crawford, G., and Botchwey, G. (2019). Unequal Extractions: Reconceptualizing the Chinese Miner in Ghana. *Labour, Capital and Society*, 49, pp. 2–29.

Loughlin, N. and Grimsditch, M. (2021). How Local Political Economy Dynamics Are Shaping the Belt and Road Initiative. *Third World Quarterly*, online first. https://doi.org/10.1080/01436597.2021.1950528.

Matković, A. (2021). Unfree Labor, from Hanoi to Belgrade: Chinese Investment and Labor Dispatch in the Case of 750 Workers from Vietnam. Institute of Economic Sciences, Belgrade.

Mertha, A. (2009). 'Fragmented Authoritarianism 2.0': Political Pluralization in the Chinese Policy Process. *The China Quarterly*, 200, pp. 995–1012.

Mueller, W. (2018). Chinese Investors in Germany: A Threat to Jobs and Labour Standards? *Made in China Journal*, 3(4), pp. 34–9.

National Development and Reform Commission, Ministry of Foreign Affairs, and Ministry of Commerce of the People's Republic of China. (2017). Vision and Action on Jointly Building Belt and Road. *Belt and Road Forum* website. http://2017.beltandroadforum.org/english/n100/2017/0410/c22-45.html.

OECD. (2018). China's Belt and Road Initiative in the Global Trade, Investment, and Finance Landscape. *OECD Business and Finance Outlook 2018*. www.oecd.org/finance/Chinas-Belt-and-Road-Initiative-in-the-global-trade-investment-and-finance-landscape.pdf.

People's Map of Global China. (2021). Hambantota Port (Magampura Mahinda Rajapaksa Port). *The People's Map of Global China*, 27 September. https://thepeoplesmap.net/project/hambantota-port-magampura-mahinda-rajapaksa-port.

Philippine Daily Inquirer. (2019). How Come There Are So Many Chinese Workers Here? *Philippine Daily Inquirer*, 7 February. www.straitstimes.com/asia/se-asia/how-come-there-are-so-many-chinese-workers-here-inquirer.

Raymond, G. (2021). From Neoliberalism to Geoeconomics: The Greater Mekong Subregion and the Archaeology of the Belt and Road Initiative in Mainland Southeast Asia. *Made in China Journal*, 6(2), pp. 152–7.

Rogelja, I. (2021). Hesteel Smederevo Steel Plant. *The People's Map of Global China*, 31 March. https://thepeoplesmap.net/project/hesteel-smederevo-steel-plant.

Schmitz, C. (2020). Doing Time, Making Money at a Chinese State Firm in Angola. *Made in China Journal*, 5(3), pp. 52–7.

Siu, P. (2019). Why Are Chinese Workers So Unpopular in Southeast Asia? *South China Morning Post*, 1 June. www.scmp.com/week-asia/politics/article/3012674/why-are-chinese-workers-so-unpopular-southeast-asia.

Smith, C. and Zheng, Y. (2016). The Management of Labour in Chinese MNCs Operating Outside of China: A Critical Review. In M. Liu and C. Smith, eds., *China at Work: A Labour Process Perspective on the Transformation of Work and Employment in China*. London: Palgrave Macmillan, pp. 361–88.

Solinger, D. (2009). *States' Gains, Labor's Losses: China, France, and Mexico Choose Global Liaisons 1980–2000*. Ithaca, NY: Cornell University Press.

Sorace, C. and Zhu, R. (2022). The Short-Lived Eternity of Friendship: Chinese Workers in Socialist Mongolia (1955–64). In I. Franceschini and C. Sorace, eds., *Proletarian China: A Century of Chinese Labour*. London: Verso Books, pp. 251–68.

Teng, W. (2019). Third World. In C. Sorace, I. Franceschini, and N. Loubere, eds., *Afterlives of Chinese Communism: Political Concepts from Mao to Xi*. London: Verso Books, pp. 281–5.

Xiao, A. H. (2015). In the Shadow of the States: The Informalities of Chinese Petty Entrepreneurship in Nigeria. *Journal of Current Chinese Affairs*, 44, pp. 75–105.

Xinhua. (2017). Visions and Actions on Jointly Building Belt and Road. *Belt and Road Forum for International Cooperation* website, 10 April. www.beltandroad2019.com/english/n100/2017/0410/c22-45.html.

Ye, M. (2019). Fragmentation and Mobilization: Domestic Politics of the Belt and Road in China. *Journal of Contemporary China*, 28(119), pp. 696–711.

Ye, M. (2020). *The Belt and Road and Beyond: State-Mobilized Globalization in China 1998–2018*. Cambridge: Cambridge University Press.

Yu, P. (2021). Letpadaung Copper Mine. *The People's Map of Global China*, 23 March. https://thepeoplesmap.net/project/letpadaung-copper-mine.

Zhang, H. (2020). The Aid-Contracting Nexus: The Role of the International Contracting Industry in China's Overseas Development Engagements. *China Perspective*, 4/2019, pp. 17–28.

Zhang, H. (2021a). Builders from China: From Third-World Solidarity to Globalised State Capitalism. *Made in China Journal*, 6(2), pp. 87–94.

Zhang, H. (2021b). Internationalization of China's Developmental State: Mechanisms and Impacts. PhD Dissertation, George Mason University.

Zhang, S. (2018). My Rights Have Been Left Behind in Papua New Guinea: The Predicament of Chinese Overseas Workers. *Made in China Journal*, 3 (3), pp. 36–9.

Zheng, Y. and Smith, C. (2017). Chinese Multinational Corporation in Europe: Racing to the Bottom? *Made in China Journal*, 2(3), pp. 26–31.

Zhu, R. (2020). The Double-Tongued Dilemma: Translating Chinese Workers' Relations in Mongolia. *Made in China Journal*, 5(3), pp. 58–65.

5 The Academe

Barkenaes, M. (2020). NYU Shanghai Students and Staff Respond to New York Post Article on School's Self-Censorship. *On Century Avenue*, 20 February. http://oncenturyavenue.org/2020/02/nyu-shanghai-students-and-staff-respond-to-new-york-post-article-on-schools-self-censorship/.

Barmé, G. R. (2012). Telling Chinese Stories. *The China Story*. www.thechinastory.org/yearbook/telling-chinese-stories.

Barry, E. (2022). 'In the End, You're Treated Like a Spy,' Says M.I.T. Scientist. *The New York Times*, 24 January. www.nytimes.com/2022/01/24/science/gang-chen-mit-china.html.

Buranyi, S. (2017). Is the Staggeringly Profitable Business of Scientific Publishing Bad for Science? *The Guardian*, 27 June. www.theguardian.com/science/2017/jun/27/profitable-business-scientific-publishing-bad-for-science.

Byler, D. (2022a). Surveillance, Data Police, and Digital Enclosure in Xinjiang 'Safe Cities'. In D. Byler, I. Franceschini, and N. Loubere, eds., *Xinjiang Year Zero*. Canberra: ANU Press, pp. 176–96.

Darrowby, J. (2019). Intellectual Property, Artificial Intelligence, and Ethical Dilemmas: China and the New Frontiers of Academic Integrity. *Made in China Journal*, 4(1), pp. 24–8.

Dunning, S., Williams, M., Geoghegan, P., and Pogrund, G. (2021). Cambridge Professor Whose Role Was 'Funded by China' Cautioned Against Uyghur Debate. *openDemocracy*, 5 June. www.opendemocracy.net/en/dark-money-investigations/cambridge-professor-role-funded-by-china-cautioned-uyghur-debate-peter-nolan.

Fisher, L. and Dunning, S. (2020). Jesus College Accepted £155,000 Contribution from Huawei. *The Times*, 10 July. www.thetimes.co.uk/article/jesus-college-accepted-155-000-contribution-from-huawei-53rr7qmcf.

Fleming, P. (2021). *Dark Academia: How Universities Die*. London: Pluto Press.

Franceschini, I. (2021). The Work of Culture: Of Barons, Dark Academia, and the Corruption of Language in the Neoliberal University. *Made in China Journal*, 6(2), pp. 241–9.

Graeber, D. (2015). *The Utopia of Rules*. New York: Melville House.

Graeber, D. (2018). *Bullshit Jobs: The Rise of Pointless Work and What We Can Do about It*. London: Penguin Books.

Greatrex, R. (2014). Letter of Protest at Interference in EACS Conference in Portugal, July 2014. *European Association for Chinese Studies* website, 30 July. http://chinesestudies.eu/?p=585.

Guardian. (2013). Sydney University Criticised for Blocking Dalai Lama Visit. *The Guardian*, 18 April. www.theguardian.com/world/2013/apr/18/sydney-university-dalai-lama.

Hayhoe, R. (1996). *China's Universities, 1895–1995: A Century of Cultural Conflict*. Abingdon, UK: Routledge.

Heckman, J. and Moktan, S. (2018). The Tyranny of the Top Five Journals. *Institute for New Economic Thinking*, 2 October. www.ineteconomics.org/perspectives/blog/the-tyranny-of-the-top-five-journals.

Hunter, F. (2019). Universities Must Accept China's Directives on Confucius Institutes, Contracts Reveal. *The Sydney Morning Herald*, 24 July. www.smh.com.au/politics/federal/universities-must-accept-china-s-directives-on-confucius-institutes-contracts-reveal-20190724-p52ab9.html.

Kennedy, M. and Phillips, T. (2017). Cambridge University Press Backs Down over China Censorship. *The Guardian*, 21 August. www.theguardian.com/education/2017/aug/21/cambridge-university-press-to-back-down-over-china-censorship.

Lattimore, O. (1950). *Ordeal by Slander*. Boston, MA: Little, Brown and Company.

Levine, J. (2019). NYU Shanghai Campus 'Self-Censoring, Politically Neutral' on Hong Kong: Faculty. *New York Post*, 19 October. https://nypost.com/2019/10/19/nyu-shanghai-campus-self-censoring-politically-neutral-on-hong-kong-faculty.

Lewis, M. K. (2021). Criminalizing China. *Journal of Criminal Law and Criminology*, 111(1), pp. 145–225.

Loubere, N. and Franceschini, I. (2017). Beyond the Great Paywall: A Lesson from the Cambridge University Press China Incident. *Made in China Journal*, 2(3), pp. 64–6.

McCoy, D. (2014). Universities Must Resist the Military Industrial Complex. *openDemocracy*, 11 March. www.opendemocracy.net/en/shine-a-light/universities-must-resist-military-industrial-complex.

McGowan, M. (2018). University Explains Why It Walked Away from Western Civilisation Degree. *The Guardian*, 5 June. www.theguardian.com/australia-news/2018/jun/06/university-explains-why-it-walked-away-from-grant-for-western-civilisation-degree.

MCLC. (2018). Protest Against Springer Bowing to Censorship, MCLC Resource Center. *MCLC Blog*, 4 October. http://u.osu.edu/mclc/2018/10/04/protest-against-springer-bowing-to-censorship.

Mehta, G. (2020). Proposal to Install Spyware in University Libraries to Protect Copyrights Shocks Academics. *Coda Story*, 13 November. www.codastory.com/authoritarian-tech/spyware-in-libraries.

Monbiot, G. (2018). Scientific Publishing Is a Rip-Off. We Fund the Research – It Should Be Free. *The Guardian*, 13 September. www.theguardian.com/commentisfree/2018/sep/13/scientific-publishing-rip-off-taxpayers-fund-research.

Murphy, S. (2017). *Zombie University: Thinking Under Control*. London: Repeater Books.

NYU Shanghai (2019). Community Standards at NYU Shanghai. *NYU Shanghai* website. https://shanghai.nyu.edu/sites/default/files/media/nyu_shanghai_community_standards_2019_2020.pdf.

Phillips, T. (2017). Cambridge University Press Accused of 'Selling Its Soul' over Chinese Censorship. *The Guardian*, 19 August. www.theguardian.com/world/2017/aug/19/cambridge-university-press-accused-of-selling-its-soul-over-chinese-censorship.

Repnikova, M. (2022). *Chinese Soft Power*. Cambridge: Cambridge University Press.

Reuters. (2017). Springer Nature Blocks Access to Certain Articles in China. *Reuters*, 1 November. www.reuters.com/article/us-china-censorship/springer-nature-blocks-access-to-certain-articles-in-china-idUSKBN1D14EB.

Sahlins, M. (2014). Confucius Institutes: Academic Malware. *The Asia-Pacific Journal: Japan Focus*, 12(46). https://apjjf.org/2014/12/46/Marshall-Sahlins/4220.html.

Sahlins, M. (2015). *Confucius Institutes: Academic Malware*. Chicago, IL: Prickly Paradigm Press.

Schuessler, J. (2021). Leader of Prestigious Yale Program Resigns, Citing Donor Pressure. *The New York Times*, 30 September. www.nytimes.com/2021/09/30/arts/yale-grand-strategy-resignation.html.

SCMP. (2017). At Beijing Book Fair, Publishers Admit to Self-Censorship. *South China Morning Post*, 24 August. www.scmp.com/news/china/policies-politics/article/2108095/beijing-book-fair-publishers-admit-self-censorship-keep.

Strelcová, A. B. (2021). The Belt and Road Initiative and the Internationalisation of Chinese Higher Education. *Made in China Journal*, 6(2), pp. 158–63.

Study Group. (n.d.). *Study Group* website. www.studygroup.com.

University of Wollongong. (2019). UOW Responds on Ramsay Centre Partnership. *University of Wollongong* website. www.uow.edu.au/the-arts-social-sciences-humanities/schools-entities/liberal-arts/faqs.

UnKoch My Campus. (n.d.). *Unkoch My Campus* website. www.unkochmy campus.org.

Washington Post. (2014). Academic Freedom Shouldn't Have a Price Tag. *The Washington Post*, 21 June. www.washingtonpost.com/opinions/the-price-of-confucius-institutes/2014/06/21/4d7598f2-f7b6-11e3-a3a5-42be35962a52_story.html.

Wright, R. (2022). Anming Hu, Professor Falsely Accused of Espionage, Reinstated by University of Tennessee. *Knoxville News Sentinel*, 3 February. https://eu.knoxnews.com/story/news/education/2022/02/03/anming-hu-reinstated-university-of-tennessee-false-espionage-charge/9008950002/.

Acknowledgements

This Element draws from our work over the past decade, so parts of it have been previously published elsewhere. We first presented the general argument in an op-ed published in the *Made in China Journal* in July 2020 under the title 'What about Whataboutism? Viral Loads and Hyperactive Immune Responses in the China Debate'. Section 2 on social credit and digital surveillance draws on an essay titled 'The Global Age of Algorithm: Social Credit and the Financialisation of Governance in China', co-authored by Nicholas Loubere and Stefan Brehm and originally published in the *Made in China Journal* in 2018. Section 3 on Xinjiang reprises arguments that we advanced in the introduction to the volume *Xinjiang Year Zero*, which we co-edited with Darren Byler and which was published by ANU Press in 2022. Parts of Section 4 on the BRI appeared in an editorial titled 'Global China beyond the Belt and Road Initiative' that Ivan Franceschini wrote for *China Perspectives* (no. 4/2020). Finally, Section 5 on academia builds on arguments we made in an op-ed published in the *Made in China Journal* in 2018 titled 'How the Chinese Censors Highlight Fundamental Flaws in Academic Publishing' and an essay titled 'The New Censorship, the New Academic Freedom: Commercial Publishers and the Chinese Market' published by Nicholas Loubere in the *Journal of the European Association for Chinese Studies*. We are grateful to all those friends and colleagues who provided feedback on earlier, partial drafts of the sections included in the Element, in particular to Darren Byler, Mark Grimsditch, Diego Gullotta, Jane Hayward, Gerald Roche, Christian Sorace, Konstantinos Tsimonis, Chenchen Zhang, and Stella Hong Zhang, as well as to the anonymous referees. Responsibility for omissions and mistakes obviously lies entirely with us. We are also thankful to Ching Kwan Lee for supporting the idea of such a book from the beginning and to the Per Anders och Maibrit Westrins Stiftelse for generous financial support to make the book Open Access.

Cambridge Elements ≡

Global China

Ching Kwan Lee
University of California, Los Angeles

Ching Kwan Lee is professor of sociology at the University of California–Los Angeles. Her scholarly interests include political sociology, popular protests, labor, development, political economy, comparative ethnography, China, Hong Kong, East Asia and the Global South. She is the author of three multiple award-winning monographs on contemporary China: *Gender and the South China Miracle: Two Worlds of Factory Women* (1998), *Against the Law: Labor Protests in China's Rustbelt and Sunbelt* (2007), and *The Specter of Global China: Politics, Labor and Foreign Investment in Africa* (2017). Her co-edited volumes include *Take Back Our Future: An Eventful Sociology of Hong Kong's Umbrella Movement* (2019) and *The Social Question in the 21st Century: A Global View* (2019).

About the Series

The Cambridge Elements series Global China showcases thematic, region- or country-specific studies on China's multifaceted global engagements and impacts. Each title, written by a leading scholar of the subject matter at hand, combines a succinct, comprehensive and up-to-date overview of the debates in the scholarly literature with original analysis and a clear argument. Featuring cutting edge scholarship on arguably one of the most important and controversial developments in the 21st century, the Global China Elements series will advance a new direction of China scholarship that expands China Studies beyond China's territorial boundaries.

Cambridge Elements ≡

Global China

Printed in the United States
by Baker & Taylor Publisher Services